SpringerBriefs in Computer Science

More information about this series at http://www.springer.com/series/10028

Hilarie Orman

Encrypted Email

The History and Technology
of Message Privacy

 Springer

Hilarie Orman
Purple Streak, Inc.
Woodland Hills, UT
USA

ISSN 2191-5768   ISSN 2191-5776 (electronic)
SpringerBriefs in Computer Science
ISBN 978-3-319-21343-9   ISBN 978-3-319-21344-6 (eBook)
DOI 10.1007/978-3-319-21344-6

Library of Congress Control Number: 2015944454

Springer Cham Heidelberg New York Dordrecht London

Printed on acid-free paper

Springer International Publishing AG Switzerland is part of Springer Science+Business Media
(www.springer.com)

Preface

Like most people, I hope that my email is only being read by the people I send it to, but I realize that my hope is unfulfilled by ordinary email technology. Though almost everyone recognizes the importance of Web site security, their email, which might be much more personal, is rarely protected. In light of the unending revelations of insecure practices by Web site owners and the general uneasiness over surveillance by governments, a few people suggested to me that email privacy would be worthwhile. I was pleased to find that almost all my computing devices had preinstalled email clients with privacy controls.

Mind you, this was not surprising to me, because I first used secure email about twenty-five years ago. I felt that I understood the underlying cryptology and Internet protocols, if not in detail, at least in general design. How hard could it be to use today's tools? I set out on my secure email adventure with as little understanding of my task as a neophyte hiker with ill-fitting boots.

As I started on the journey, I made many informal queries among security-conscious, computer-savvy people about their use of encrypted email. Few of them had much experience with it, and it seemed that those with the most background had the most negative opinions. "Is it really that bad?" I wondered.

My first experiences were positive. Almost all the email systems that I had access to were supplied with software for encrypting and signing messages. It was a little bit difficult to find out where the controls were (hint: find the "Advanced" tab), and for some of them, I had to download additional software, but overall it went well. Then, I had to approach the problem of getting keys and configuring my email readers to use them. This presented some challenges, and I stumbled here and there, finally reaching a satisfactory state.

A stranger in a strange land, I found no one to share my adventure. Even though I correspond regularly with experts in computer security, no one I knew was interested in exchanging secure email. Checking over several years of past email, I could see little evidence that anyone I knew had the necessary prerequisite of the all-important public key: Fewer than one person in a thousand used the simple and unobtrusive signed email. I implored a few people to take the secure email plunge. Some initial experiments went awry, and I had to convince my correspondents to keep trying to find the magic controls for accepting my keys, and I had to accept their keys. Strange error messages ensued. We forged on.

The experience was like treading over a rocky and distorted landscape without GPS. In each case, I reached my goal, but I began to understand how this technology that started out so bravely 25 years ago had shifted, fractured, and bent to become a frustrating terrain. I hope that those who read this book will understand the geology of the landscape and the well-trodden trails so that they can become skilled users of secure email and trail guides for their correspondents.

This is not a cookbook for using secure email nor a guide to buying a commercial email product. Such an effort would have to encompass too many email systems and key management utilities. What I have tried to accomplish is to show that underneath all the menus and tabs, there is machinery that carries out an understandable process of building secure messages and processing them on receipt. With this background, the various email systems make sense, and when things go wrong, the oddly terse error messages can lead to solutions for otherwise frustrating problems.

Beyond being not-a-cookbook, this is not primer on cryptography. There is material that explains some basic concepts, particularly how security depends on keys and why there are different kinds of keys. Understanding these concepts makes it easier to understand why there are so many choices to be made when one first embarks on the secure email adventure.

Many people helped me uncover the early history of email encryption. Marv Schaefer, Dennis Branstad, Ruth Nelson, Steve Kent, Ray Tomlinson, Dave Dyer, Doug Dodds, and Austin Henderson helped me uncover the all-but-forgotten history of BBN's encrypted email. Matt Bishop remembered the Unix public key message utility and its inner workings. Dave Balenson was generous in sharing his briefing materials and recollections of the IETF standards developed in the 1980s and 1990s. Jim Galvin's recollections about the IETF standards were equally generous and helpful. Mark Feldman provided archives of the PEM developers' email list from the 1990s.

Jon Callas was patient and helpful in answering my questions about the PGP specification and its interpretation. Tolga Acar had helpful observations about a popular email application. Don Cohen helped with my encrypted email experiments.

Richard Schroeppel was ever present to answer all my mathematical questions and made countless cups of coffee and scoured Utah County for good take-out food to sustain the two of us during the endeavor of writing this book.

Contents

Chapter 1
Introduction: What Is Secure Email?

Almost everyone on the planet gets messages delivered by the Internet in one form or another. Email, text messages, social media—these all allow a person to send a message to another person easily and quickly. The paradigm is remarkably similar to that ancient and fast-disappearing paper-based communication form: the postal service aka "snail mail". On the outside of an envelope, you write the name and address of the intended recipient, and you usually put your own name and address on the envelope. Inside the envelope is the message, whatever it might be. The postal service delivers the message. In theory, an undamaged envelope is assurance that the message was not opened.

Electronic communication is similar, but much faster, and the envelopes are essentially transparent. We hope that no one is eavesdropping on our email, but it can and does happen, sometimes with embarrassing consequences. Just as with ordinary paper mail, electronic mail is not delivered immediately to the recipient; it goes through intermediate stops before being deposited somewhere near the addressee. The intermediate stopping points are mail servers. The servers decide how to route the mail and where to store it when it arrives. Few people have their email delivered to their own computer these days. We want the convenience of having web-based access to the email no matter where we are. We entrust our email storage to Google via gmail.com, or to Yahoo, or our employer, or our Internet Service Provider (ISP). None of these places gives us absolute assurance that our email is protected from all prying eyes. Their system administrators, their network administrators, authorized law enforcement officials, and observers using undetected malware, can all read the email.

Security-conscious email providers do take precautions to shield the email while it is in transit between intermediaries, and they do use cryptography to protect the communication between a user and the email server. This could be compared to keeping postal delivery trucks and mail carrier delivery bags under lock and key. It is good, but every system has its lapses due to error or malfeasance, and the user must depend on many cogs working together perfectly to keep his email secure.

Internet security guidance has made users cognizant of the importance of the padlock icon in their browser, indicating their connection to a website is "secure". There is a lot of software that goes into implementing the cryptographic algorithms that give meaning to that padlock, and almost all of it was originally designed for

© The Author(s) 2015
H. Orman, *Encrypted Email*,
SpringerBriefs in Computer Science,
DOI 10.1007/978-3-319-21344-6_1

email systems. Thus, the fundamental underpinnings of secure email are commonly available in software libraries, and making it available to email applications is entirely feasible. As a result, although few people are using cryptography to keep their email private, it can be done. Almost all major email handling systems support confidentiality and authentication. The two features are there, lurking under obscure menu options, waiting to be used.

Email security means several things. First, we want to know that email we receive has not been read by anyone else. Of course, the sender knows what the message is, and perhaps other people were copied by the sender, but we expect the intentions of the sender to be honored during the delivery process. In the other direction, we want the same assurance when we send email. This property is what we call "privacy" or "confidentiality". Secondly, we would like to be sure that this is the message that was actually composed by the sender. If even the tiniest part of the message was changed between the time it was sent and the time we received it, there should be some way of knowing. This is called "message modification detection" or "integrity protection".

Another assurance that is often important is knowing who sent the message. Not just who seems to have sent it, but who *really* sent it. We have all seen email messages that purport to come from our ISP or a social network site, but the messages really are sent by shadowy advertisers. The property of being able to associate an identity with a message is called "authentication". One of the great cryptographic discoveries of the 20th century was how to do this mathematically.

For some people, authentication is as important, perhaps more important, than privacy. For example, someone who posts information on a social media site or a public email list may be concerned about attribution. Reputations can be ruined over a gaffe, but if the offending remark was actually sent by a rival masquerading as the victim, the victim can land in hot water in an instant. If all mail were authenticated with cryptography, this problem would diminish. In another context, an employee might be reluctant to take an action demanded in an email without knowing that his supervisor was truly the sender.

Most email systems can protect a message with confidentiality alone, authentication alone, or both. These protections are usually called "encryption" and "signing". When messages are received, the recipient's email handler reverses the operations by decryption to make the message readable and/or checking that the signature is from the purported sender ("verification").

Often, this all works seamlessly. More often, each pair of users will go through some amount of struggle to align the necessary resources for seamless operation. Subsequent chapters will show how two differing philosophies about "trust" brought secure email to its present state, how today's secure email systems can be used effectively, and how advanced users can get extra benefits from the myriad of software features that are packed into the systems.

What Is End-to-End Encryption?

The strongest guarantees of email security depend on complete control of the cryptographic keys being in the hands of the senders and receivers. That is the only way to achieve seamless cryptographic protections from the beginning to end of the email delivery process—end-to-end. Any other methods result in dependencies on third-party practices, intentions, and legal requirements.

Quite a lot of encryption has made its way into the Internet, and much of our communication is private. Email has a couple of unique requirements. For commercial transactions, our identity is not as important as is the ability to effect payment. It is critically important that a customer know that he is interacting with a legitimate, soundly identified company through its website, and the customer also needs to be sure that his credit card information cannot be seen by eavesdroppers. Email, on the other hand, is sent through intermediaries that can see the contents.

The Internet email protocol design assumes that an email message is destined to be delivered to a software agent, and the recipient will see the message at some convenient time. Typically, when you send an email, it goes from your computer to a mail server at your Internet Service Provider's facility. From there, the server will send it to a mail server associated with the recipient's address. It might be "mail.example.com" or "gmail.com". And from there it might be routed through other servers, before coming to rest either on the computer of the recipient, or on a computer that he can access through a local mail transfer protocol such as POP3 or IMAP.

During all these transfers, the message acquires more and more headers showing its path; if you look at the "with headers" or similar option in a mail reader, you'll see the Internet names of the servers that have handled the message before you got it. Is your mail private if that many other computers have seen it? The providers will argue that they take many precautions to protect their customers' communication. These are laudable efforts, but they are piecemeal solutions that are not visible to the customers. The messages might have been protected or not, there is no way of knowing.

Most email providers have encrypted links connecting their servers, so the messages are not visible to eavesdroppers on the communication lines. There is an IETF standard for secure connections between servers [14]. The need for it came to public attention when Edward Snowden released documents showing that the US government was aware that Google's network of servers did not use encryption to protect its communication lines. According to Snowden, agents of the US government recorded data from those lines without Google's knowledge.

The confidentiality of email is best assured by encrypting the messages at the point of origin (the sender's computer) and decrypting by the recipient. This is called "end-to-end" encryption, and it is the only way for the sender and receiver to control the security of their email with certainty. Anything else relies on the competence and trustworthiness of other parties.

Many email providers today will claim that they have "second generation" secure email. In a second generation system, the email is generally held in encrypted form on a server, perhaps part of the "cloud". When the user logs into his cloud account, his email is decrypted with his private key, on the server, and transmitted over secure communication channels to his current computing device. This has the advantage of keeping the data secure on the server, but it still means that the user's private key must be available to the server machine. The second generation systems are a good compromise, but they are short of the full security of end-to-end methods.

End-to-end encryption is a panacea with headaches. The messages cannot be read without the correct private key. Moving the private key to all the devices that might read email is a problem that is getting more difficult as we increase the number and variety of computing devices that we carry around. This is why the biggest problem that a new user will encounter is reading email on a mobile device and discovering that he does not have the private key for reading encrypted messages that he might have received.

Drawbacks:

1. The senders and receivers must manage keys for themselves and their contacts.
2. The email folders cannot be searched by a remote server.
3. Mobile device email apps might not support end-to-end, or have bugs.
4. Web-based email readers cannot support end-to-end cryptography without a complicated browser plug-in.
5. You cannot read encrypted email that you have sent unless you use "cc" to send a copy to yourself.
6. The fact that email is encrypted is evident to anyone who sees the email; if you think that you might be targeted for surveillance simply because you use email security features, there is little that you can do to hide the fact.

None of these problems is insurmountable, but they have an impact on usability that is often daunting. Subsequent chapters will attempt to illuminate the way encrypted email works in several scenarios. By showing how things work, we hope to make the entire process more understandable. Some of the barriers to widespread adoption of email security are simply those of familiarity, and once over the numerous hurdles, most people will begin to find security is a normal part of their technological life.

The (Slippery) Meaning of Trust

Secure email is a way of using cryptography to increase trust in Internet communication. The basis for the trust is confidence in the mathematics of cryptography and the software that implements it. Over the past 50 years the academic world has produced a wealth of methods and theoretical analyses that contribute to that confidence. It is important to understand the foundations for it, and how that technology interacts with the more traditional notions of trust. There are fine points both to the definition of trust and to privacy, and it is important that users understand them when they choose the cryptographic enhancements for their secure email messages.

The Internet is a place where you can meet many people. If you care enough about your communication with them to use email security features, then you have some reason to trust them, and they probably have some reason to trust you. Here the word "trust" means the subjective, intangible concept of human trust. Once an email message has been composed and you are ready to send it to the person you trust, the confidentiality of that message comes down to the very tangible quantity that is the public key you associate with the email address for that person. This simple association can turn into a big management problem.

Let us assume that Alice has sent Bob an encrypted email. If Bob can successfully decrypt it, and he sees that it is from Alice, how can he relate his human trust of Alice into some kind of trust of the message? Because the public key belongs to Bob, there is no assurance that Alice sent the message. However, Bob does know that an eavesdropper could not have read the message because he has kept his private key securely stored (we hope!). If the message sounds like it came from Alice, then Bob may trust the message based on his human understanding of Alice and her communication style.

There is one other thing that Bob should be able to count on, and that is the "integrity" of the message. Did someone tamper with the message before he read it? That should be impossible if there is a "modification detection code (MDC)" as part of what he received. It is a common mistake to think that encryption by itself scrambles a message in a way that makes it impossible to modify the result without destroying the whole message when it is decrypted. In fact, it is entirely possible to modify the encrypted data; the receiver will see the parts preceding the modification without any problem, but the parts subsequent to the modification might look strange. This fact complicates cryptographic practice; including an MDC lets the sender detect tampering. An MDC is a one-way function of the message, and Bob can use that function to make sure that the MDC value that he received is the one that matches the message he received.

Bob now has a message that he believes was sent to him privately and was not modified, but he has no mathematical basis for tying the message to the purported sender, Alice. For many people, this is sufficient, and they are happy enough to carry on a conversation. Bob may use his human understanding of context to establish trust. Suppose that Alice has sent him a message with the text "The report has an error on page 5 where you state 'the valve is shut'", and he uses Alice's public key to send the reply, "Your comment about the valve, on page 5, is confusing. What did you mean?", and Alice replies "The valve comment on page 5 should not confuse you, it is wrong because the system is down for maintenance". In Bob's mind, only Alice could have read the message that he sent about his confusion about the valve, and he reply shows that received it. Their communication is private, because it is protected by their private keys, and thus, they have a human reason to believe that they are communicating with the correct person.

It would be relatively easy for anyone to send Bob an encrypted email, purporting to be from Alice, with similar messages. How much context is enough to reassure Bob? Someone who has a detailed knowledge of their activities might successfully intervene in their conversation. "I want to delete all mention of valves from the report—Alice" reads a message to Bob. Should he trust it or not? Bob needs a mathematical reason to believe that messages are from Alice.

Public keys provide a solution to Bob's dilemma through signatures. A public key signature is a mathematical way for Alice to let Bob know that a message really came from her. Alice creates a one-way function of her message text (a "digest") and uses her private key to sign that quantity. She then sends this with her message to Bob. Upon receiving this, Bob can decrypt the message, check that the signature on the digest really is signed by Alice. Then he has a mathematical reasons to support four important claims: the messages was not exposed to eavesdroppers, the message was intended for him, the message has not been modified, and Alice sent the message.

Other Qualities

There are many other things that Bob and Alice might want to know about their email—Did Alice receive Bob's message? At what time? Did she decrypt and read it? Did she forward it to someone else? These are important properties of message security, and it is possible to achieve them and more if Alice and Bob have trustworthy software running on their computing devices. Extra assurance would be gained if they could prove to one another that their computing devices were built from circuits that were provably correct. These properties are far removed from the basic properties that public keys and encipherment provide, and there is no readily available software that incorporates them into email systems. There is one property, though, that is controversial, and different scenarios require different approaches: non-repudiation.

The "non-repudiation" question are these: Can Bob prove to Carol that he received a particular message from Alice? Can an eavesdropper see that Alice has sent a particular message to Bob? These questions couple authentication and privacy in a way that can be uncomfortable. For a contract, there are legal reasons for establishing the first property, but in truly private person-to-person communication, it is not necessary. In fact, Alice might not want Bob to be able to prove that he has communicated with her because such a disclosure might be harmful to them both.

Some people argue that Internet email headers reveal the sender and receiver, but that is not the whole story with respect to privacy. If Alice signs a message as the last step in message preparation, and if she signs something observable by an eavesdropper, then that eavesdropper can try to verify that the observable data was signed by her public key. But Alice might be playing a game of hide-and-seek in which she sends the data from her email account "alice@example.com" but signs it with a key for her alter ego "alice@wonderland-lewiscarrol.com". Although her public key for the latter identity is available in public databases, she does not want anyone to know that the two "alices" are one and the same.

In another scenario, a third party, say Dave demands to know if Bob has received email from Alice. "No," says Bob. But Dave looks at the encrypted email on Bob's webserver and sees that one message is signed by Alice. "Aha, you do know Alice" he declaims. To obscure this information, Alice should have hidden her signature inside something encrypted in Bob's encryption key. But this means that Bob has to decrypt the message before he is sure that it is from Alice. This is a problem for people who do not want to have data from untrusted correspondents on their machines.

People have come up with many more security properties that that would be useful for email. The first team of people who undertook to define email security for the Internet mentioned several of them [22]:

1. access control,
2. traffic flow confidentiality,
3. address list accuracy,
4. routing control,
5. issues relating to the casual serial reuse and sharing of personal computing devices or computers in public spaces by multiple users,
6. assurance of message receipt and non-deniability of receipt,
7. automatic association of acknowledgments with the messages to which they refer, and
8. message duplicate detection, replay prevention, or other stream-oriented services.

These things are difficult to implement and not generally demanded, and so they remain options that some email systems might implement for their own set of users, but they are not universally available. Today we might add even more desiderata, including the ability to search for keywords in encrypted email, to selectively share parts of encrypted messages, to have notary services for email, and to have a secure timestamping service. However, none of these have universal applicability, and there are not enough compelling reasons today to add any of them to commonly available software bases.

Chapter 2
A Brief History of Secure Email

Though language is a universal human trait, written language has a much shorter history with our species. It does seem clear from archaeological records that humans have a fascination with symbols. Symbols acquire associated meanings over time, but only those who are familiar with the context understand what those meanings are. We know little about the meaning of the Neanderthal cave drawings other than that they have something to do with animals that could be hunted with primitive weapons.

Eventually symbols became a way of representing words, and written language emerged. There is a paradox with the written word. It does not come naturally to us, it must be taught separately from spoken language, which we seem to pick up without instruction. Written language is mysterious to children, as it is to primitive peoples.

> Whence did the wondrous mystic art arise
> Of painting speech, and speaking to the eyes?
> That we by magic lines are taught,
> How both to color and embody thought?

[Oft quoted historically, but source unknown]

At first, written language must have been secret in itself because so few people knew how to read. As civilization spread, people relied more and more on the written word for record keeping and communication across distance. Reading became common enough that it was not private, but the need for privacy became if anything, even more important. Roman military leaders are credited with the first uses of encryption for communication privacy [16].

But cryptography did not catch on the way written language did, and there is little evidence of its use as Europe endured the Dark Ages. Finally, in the 1200s, along with the rise of trade and increased communication via letters, cryptography found a permanent niche with the "flowering of modern diplomacy." [16, pg. 108] Since then, cryptology grown in importance, finally exploding into practical use on the Internet starting in the 1990s.

Kahn [16], the Codebreakers, page 91: "... cryptology was acquiring a taint that lingers even today—the conviction in the minds of many people that cryptology is a black art, a form of occultism whose practitioner must, in William F. Friedman's

© The Author(s) 2015
H. Orman, *Encrypted Email*,
SpringerBriefs in Computer Science,
DOI 10.1007/978-3-319-21344-6_2

apt phrase, "perforce commune daily with dark spirits to accomplish his feats of mental jui-jitsu."

At the dawn of time in the computer era, there was no email and there was no Internet. There were few computers, and there were computer programs, and people used the computers for different tasks, but there were no identifiable "users". Sending a message to another user made no sense if there was only one person at a time using the computer. Yet, because computers were so expensive and so useful, by the 1960's, there were a few computers capable of running software programs for several simultaneous users. This efficiency created a more productive environment for software development. These shared computers sprouted the seeds of email.

One early system was the time-sharing computer developed by System Development Corporation [21]. As part of a demonstration, they arranged to use three computers in three different cities. Their task was to demonstrate that data could be copied from one computer to another using phone lines for communication. The three development teams needed work together, and they came up with the idea of sending messages to each other. At first, they simply sent messages to their computer operator when they needed administrative actions like "let my program run for the next 10 min" and the operator might reply "ok, the program is running now". The messages in those days were printed on teletypes, and the operator probably knew only which teletype would print the message, not which person would read it. The developers added the capability of sending messages from one teletype to another, and this might have been the first demonstration of remote computer messaging.

As the number of computers grew, the number of users increased. The diversity of work done on a single computer increased, and administrators wanted to know who used the computer and individuals wanted to keep their data separated from the data of others. Soon the time-sharing computers began assigning "usernames". The messaging idea quickly extended to user-to-user messages in which the sender was identified by username preceding the message.

In technical terms, a message was a way to send keystrokes from one computer terminal to another, but only if the intended user was at the terminal. So being "logged in" meant sitting at sending and printing device like a teletype, or as became more and more common, a cathode ray tube with text display.

Suppose the person you wanted to communicate with was not logged in? In that case, the messaging software could create a file with the message in it, and when the user did log in, the operating system would let him know that the message was waiting for him. Oddly enough, the idea of attaching the sender's name to the message wasn't always part of the messaging paradigm.

Despite the primitive nature of early messaging, it was useful enough to become an expected attribute of an operating system. Almost as soon as the ARPANET (the precursor to the Internet) was developed, messaging was extended to allow users on different machines to send messages to one another. These early systems were idiosyncratic with respect to the form of an email address, but they allowed people on opposite sides of the country to plan where to go to dinner when developers traveled to meet their colleagues at other facilities.

By the mid 1970's most of the attributes of modern email systems were incorporated into software systems. The "@" form of addressing became universal, and messages had subjects, senders, cc's, and messages could be saved for later reading.

Very little of the information on early computers was private. If you were using a time-sharing system you had to trust your colleagues not to pry or steal or destroy your data. Even after systems like Multics and Unix added access control settings for files and software, people understood that the system administrators had access to all their data.

In 1973 Roger Shell added file encryption to the Multics operating system. A user could choose a key, enter it into the encryption program, and have his file encrypted with that key. The user could decrypt it if he entered the same key as he had for encryption. The cipher was one designed by Shell, and its design was an innovative one for that era, using data dependent rotations, among other things. Multics had user-to-user messaging and email, but encryption was not extended to those functions.

Strong protections for email were considered in the 1970s when an ARPA project sought ways to use the early Internet for classified military messages. The Military Messaging Experiment (MME) [17] defined a formal model of classification labels built into an ARPANET message handling system running on the BBN TENEX operating system. Although the MME did not envision or specify software encryption, Austin Henderson of BBN, on his own initiative, added symmetric encryption to the Hermes message handling system around 1974 [6]. Hermes was part of the normal TENEX system, and many people used it, not just those who were part of MME. This was probably the first time that email was encrypted. The Hermes system prompted the user for a text string to use as starting material for a key, that text was scrambled to form an encryption key K; then message was encrypted with key K. The resulting data was converted to an ascii text format (blocks of 5 letters separated by spaces), and it was sent using the email system. The recipient was prompted for the key, and the whole process was reversed to reveal the plaintext.

Of course, key management had to be done on an ad hoc basis. Symmetric key algorithms require that the sender and receiver share the same key, and it is difficult for two parties to agree on a key without meeting in person or making a phone call.

Fortunately, the key management problem was on the cusp of a huge change.

The Public Key Era Begins

In 1976 a group of researchers developed the idea of public key cryptography [8]. It was a brilliant discovery that established a demarcation point in the history of the field. Before public key, when two parties needed to communicate, they had to have some secure channel to let each other know what their cipher key would be. They might meet in person and tell each other, or they might agree to use some common information from a newspaper (for example, the closing value of the stock market from the previous day), or they could establish a code, using either a code book or a convention such as 4267 meaning "the 4th word from the top of page 267 in the Merriam Webster dictionary of 1952." Key distribution was the Achilles heel of cryptography.

The astonishing contribution of public key cryptography was to let a person give one key to *everyone* and say "use this key to encrypt messages to me". With symmetric key cryptography, this would be silly because the same key that encrypts messages is the one that decrypts messages. Anyone who had the key could decrypt any messages sent to you. But with public key cryptography, the encryption key is not the decryption key. Only you know the decryption key corresponding to your own encryption key, and only you can decrypt the messages sent to you.

Public key cryptography depends on finding a function that is easy to compute if you know some extra information, but is very hard to compute otherwise. One simple way to do this is with modular exponentiation of large numbers. The word "modular" means using "clock arithmetic". In the explanations of public key methods, the notation "x mod n" means the remainder of "x" divided by "n". Mathematicians have long known that raising a number to a power using modular arithmetic is an interesting operation. For example, if p is an odd prime number and n is an integer, then there are numbers g that have the property that ad n range from 1 to $p-1$, the values of

$$g^n \bmod p$$

are all the numbers from 1 to $p - 1$ in some order. Numbers like g are called generators.

Another interesting property is the commutative property:

$$\left(g^a\right)^b = g^{ab} = \left(g^b\right)^a \bmod p$$

This leads to the elegant Diffie-Hellman key exchange method. If Alice and Bob and others have agreed to use a very large prime number p and a generating number g as their secret scheme, then they can choose secret numbers and publish public keys. Alice will tell people that her public key is the number $g^a mod\, p$ and Bob will tell people that his public key is the number $g^b mod\, p$, but each of them keeps their exponent as a secret. Then when Bob and Alice want to establish a secret number between themselves, they can both calculate g^{ab} and use that as the basis for enciphering their messages. No one else can calculate the secret exponents, even if they know the public values, because the problem of going from $g^x mod\, p$ to x is very difficult.

Shortly thereafter, a trio of MIT professors found a mathematical algorithm for public key cryptography [27], and the RSA algorithm became one of the most famous mathematical methods of computer science. The algorithm is simplicity itself. Assuming that a message M is a number (in a computer, everything is a number), then the encryption of M is the following calculation:

$$enc(M) = M^e \bmod n$$

where n is the product of two large primes and e is a number called the encryption exponent. The number n and the exponent e are called the public key. For each e, there is a corresponding secret number d that will decrypt a message. The decryption exponent is the private key.

$$(enc(M))^d \bmod n = M$$

Not only does RSA enable public key encryption, it also has a flip side that serves as an authentication signature. Reversing the designation of of "public" and "private" for d and e, we obtain:

$$sign(M) = M^d \bmod n$$

The "encryption exponent" e will "encrypt" the signature and produce the original message, thus verifying that the message was signed by someone who knows secret number d corresponding to the public number e. This is the technical of "verification" in public key systems.

With these wonderful inventions, it seemed a small step to bring cryptography to bear on its natural application in email, but in 1976 there wasn't much interest. The algorithms stressed the computing capabilities of CPUs at the time. Besides, for the most part, people who used the Internet trusted one another, and they were much more interested in promulgating information than in hiding it. This is one of the conundrums that surrounds cryptography: the suspicion that it stirs up, "What are you trying to hide?" In fact, there is very little evidence that Internet users wanted secrecy. Schell's file encryption for Multics [30] is one of the few early examples of an operating system utility for cryptographic protection for data. Nonetheless, interest in privacy and security was building steadily.

In 1980, Peter Deutsch at Bell Labs develop a user-to-user messaging system that used a public key algorithm. He used Merkle's knapsack method [24] for the functions xsend and xget. If a user wanted to send an encrypted message to another (say Alice wanted to send to Bob), then Alice would use xsend, and that program would look in Bob's home directory to see if he had a public key in a file with a well-known name. The xsend program would take Bob's public key and use it to encrypt Alice's message, and then the resulting data would be put into Bob's incoming message directory. When Bob wanted to read a message, he would use the xget program, and that would use the private part of his key to decrypt the file containing the message. As luck would have it, the knapsack algorithm was flawed, and this early example of secure messaging sank from view.

Interest in cryptography was sparked by two events: the publication of the NIST standard for commercial cryptography the DES cipher [5] (first proposed around 1975), and the aforementioned discovery of public key cryptography. During this time, the Internet was becoming an essential resource for communication in the scientific community, and email systems grew from being an ad hoc collection of simple messages into an IETF standard with many independent systems for handling an ever-growing volume of messages.

By the mid 1980 s the US DoD was interested in building a secure network for military use. The Secure Data Network System (SDNS) [25] contract was awarded to several companies, including GTE. Ruth Nelson of the GTE's Electronic Defense Communications Division served as chair of the working group that defined an end-to-end encryption architecture. Their specifications for network level security were called SP3 and SP4, and they were supposed to be accompanied by a messaging protocol that would have defined secure email. However, the project's first phase ended with secure messaging remaining undone. Nevertheless, the work did provide means and impetus to explore the use of cryptography on the Internet at a time when cryptography was becoming a controversial political subject, as the US government was leery of letting the technology escape the country.

Applied cryptography on the Internet began with the Military Message Experiment [17], followed by the Secure Data Network System. In parallel, the telecommunications industry planned to be part of the networking industry. It pursued this plan through the International Standards Organization (ISO), and also through the International Telecommunications Union, a United Nations agency specializing in communication and information technologies. The ITU's consultive committee (the CCITT, later named the ITU-T), the industry produced the X.400 and X.500 [29] standards for network messages and directory services. Their joint ISO/ITU work was called the Open Systems Interconnections (OSI) protocols. Security was part of the OSI work, and the standards for encrypted content, such as network packets, were part of X.400. Those standards influenced subsequent work and were adopted for the US Department of Defense information systems. Ultimately, the DOD adopted a secure email system based on the X.400 work. The X.500 specification dealt with directory services, and one of its goals was to develop a directory structure specifically for public keys.

With the impetus of the SDNS contract, the IETF formed a Privacy Task Force (later the Privacy and Security Research Group) that quickly focused on defining standards for secure email. Their starting point was the X.400 and X.500 specifications. One of the questions they confronted was how to assign trust to a public key. While X.400 at that time specified how to use cryptography for networking, it did not yet address the problems of "interpersonal messages"—finding the private key of the recipient, how to identify which keys belonged to which people, etc. The X.500 directory services were meant to solve that problem, and part of the X.500 specification covered exactly how to identify who owned a key.

The X.400 specification was published in 1984 as "The Red Book", describing secure networking over the OSI transport model, and four years later the X.500 services group produced a standard for representing public keys and their owners. This was X.509, the certificate data structure that underlies today's website security and the S/MIME secure email standards. But in those early days of the Internet, X.509 seemed more like a solution looking for a problem.

PKI: What's Around a Name?

There is a fundamental philosophical schism that divides practitioners of authentication. That disagreement is so deep that it split secure email development into two camps.

It begins with an insight that an MIT undergraduate [19] had shortly after the RSA public key algorithm was published. Public keys are a wonderful way to start secure communication, but how can you find out what someone's public key is? Two people could send email to one another, each one showing a number that was their own public key. But how would the recipient be *sure* that it was the right key? The key might be sent by an imposter. How could you really entrust secret information to a key that arrived out of the blue? Short of meeting in person to exchange the information, could two people find a safe way to learn each other's keys?

The insight into a solution could be found in the public keys themselves. If there were a trustworthy person who could take on the task of having users validate their identities, then that trustworthy person could use his own public key to sign the binding between a person's identity and public key. The public key of the trustworthy person (or organization) could be one that was well-advertised on several reputable public websites. The signed data objects would have a binding between an "identity" (such as an ordinary name and/or an email address) and a public key. The signature of the trustworthy entity would mean "The trustworthy entity says 'this number is the public key of bob@example.com'". This simple method of authentication allowed the public keys to be freed from public directories. The keys could be stored anywhere, and they could be fetched without the need for secure communication. The signed objects, once retrieved, could be sent from person-to-person, stored on other directory servers, and yet still be verified by anyone.

But what is a name? It could be a person's ordinary legal name, an email address, or a combination of name and an organization that person belongs to—a family, a business, a school, or any number of other things. But in X.509, names identify people who have a role in a legal entity of some kind. This kind of name structure probably came into being because governments or government funded organizations designed the OSI standards. Of course, even before that, the original funding for secure messaging on the Internet came from the US Department of Defense. Their funding for the Military Message Experiment sought to embed the DoD's practice of assigning classification levels to messages, something that was eventually modeled on computer systems as the Bell-Lapadula model [3]. Besides strict ideas about message classification, the military has longstanding notions of where people belong in a hierarchy. Each member of the military is assigned to an organization within a command hierarchy, and every person has a rank within their organization. Most governments and businesses also have hierarchies, but they are often less strict about their exact memberships and how people and organizations get assigned. Outside of these formal organizations, people have even less formal designations such as friend, cousin, colleague, neighbor. The Internet brought another degree of "fuzzy" relationship to the table: people who never met in person but corresponded through

Internet email lists, bulletin boards, etc. These Internet associates might never know each other's "true names", yet they would be familiar with their opinions, preferences, and style of speech.

The X.509 system specified a way of describing a person's identity and place in a hierarchy. Along with that identifying information, there could be a public key for communicating with them confidentially. In a hierarchical organization, there must be some entity that it is responsible for identifying its members, and that is where public keys found yet another role. If each organization had a public key for signatures, then each person's directory information could be signed by the organization they belonged to. Furthermore, each organization's key could be published and signed by the organization above it in the hierarchy. At the very top of the hierarchy, one organization, the "root" would be the ultimate trusted authority.

The hierarchical structure fit naturally into governmental and corporate organizational charts. This attractiveness led to an expectation that public key technology could be an easy add-on to existing email systems. Looking up an email address and looking up a public key should be tied together into one, simple operation. That fact that this would be simple is embodied in the set of public key management operations that has come to be known as "Public Key Infrastructure" or PKI [1].

There was another aspect of certificate hierarchies that appealed to many people but repelled others. For most purposes we expect to know the "real" identity of an Internet correspondent. There is, after all, a real person sending the email, or at least an identifiable organization. For many purposes, though, the real identity is not important, and we are happy to accept a pseudonym as a reasonable identity. The practice is, of course, well established for publishing. The IETF's Privacy Task Force became the Privacy and Security Research Group (PSRG), and the members participated in discussions about what identity services to provide for secure email. Two camps emerged. One favored the idea that all identities had to be vouched for by some identifiable organization, and all organizations must be part of a hierarchy. Only a few organizations could be trusted to be "roots" of certificate hierarchies. Indeed, some people felt that the very idea of obscured identities was objectionable. Another camp recognized a need for anonymity in political discussion, and for them, the hierarchy structure looked suspiciously like de facto government controls on identity.

Secure Email Begins to Emerge

Privacy Enhanced Mail (PEM) Standardization, Part I

The PSRG moved towards defining its version of secure email [18]. The design team chose the hierarchical X.509 certificate structure as the basis for representing the binding between an identity and a public key. Not everyone was happy with the X.509 decision. Besides the argument over naming hierarchies, licensing issues dogged the requisite public key technology.

From about 1984 through 1992, the PSRG worked on defining secure email. Their work eventually was named "Privacy Enhanced Mail" (PEM). The X.400 messaging standards were the starting point for design, even though those standards were concerned with network packet and stream communication, not email.

The main technical problems to be solved by PEM were:

- to carry encrypted messages over the Internet's normal email protocol, SMTP, without changing any of the servers that forwarded email messages between sites
- use public key methods to ensure that only the intended recipient could read the message
- use public key methods to assure the authenticity of email messages
- ensure that any modifications to the message could be detected by the receiver
- facilitate the transmission of public keys

The first documents covering secure email on the Internet were issued in 1987 by the Privacy Task Force. The document was revised in subsequent years. The first version did not mention certificates, but from 1988 onward certificates were required.

PEM needed to introduce new email headers for naming the sender and receiver. Ordinary "From:" and "To:" headers do not carry enough information to unambiguously determine the public keys, so PEM added their own headers, encapsulated within the PEM message itself. PEM users could send entire certificates chains in the "X-Sender-ID" field, thus solving one of the nagging problems of public key management: how to find the keys. There were no universal directory services on the Internet, and the best way of bootstrapping the keys was to send them in email messages. This was supposed to be a temporary measure while people waiting for directory services. At the time, directory services were widely anticipated, and there were many efforts to build them based on the X.500 specifications or related work in the IETF. Yet even today, the only universal directory service is the Domain Name System (DNS).

PEM headers also carried the information about the public key algorithm, the message digest function, and the symmetric encryption algorithm. The system was "crypto agile" in that it did not have fixed algorithms built into the protocol. Instead, it anticipated that advances in cryptography would lead to changes or variety in algorithms.

To achieve these goals, PEM defined three kinds of secure messages—MIC-CLEAR, MIC, and PRIVATE. "MIC" stood for "message integrity check". MIC-CLEAR was a message that could be read without special software, but it also contained a public key signature tying the sender's identity to the message; MIC, on the other hand, had a more robust message representation encoding that was less susceptible to in-transit modifications that would cause the signature verification to fail. PRIVATE messages were encrypted with the public key of the recipient and then encoded into 80 character lines of ascii characters.There were ultimately four documents that defined PEM

RFC 1421 Privacy Enhancement for Internet Electronic Mail: Part I: Message Encryption and Authentication Procedures	1993–02
RFC 1422 Privacy Enhancement for Internet Electronic Mail: Part II: Certificate-Based Key Management	1993–02
RFC 1423 Privacy Enhancement for Internet Electronic Mail: Part III: Algorithms, Modes, and Identifiers	1993–02
RFC 1424 Privacy Enhancement for Internet Electronic Mail: Part IV: Key Certification and Related Services	1993–02

Beyond these 4 documents, there were also 3 that defined modification detection algorithms: MD2, MD4, and MD5 [28]. Each method had been designed by Ron Rivest, and they reflected different balances between security and speed. None of these are considered secure today, but they were state of the art at the time.

Trusted Information Systems, a small security company in Glenwood, Maryland, developed software that implemented PEM. It ran on PCs and was integrated into the MH email system on Unix. The PEM software issued certificates for a list of users who were enrolled by an administrator, and the certificates were delivered to the users via an initial request message and reply.

The PEM designers deliberately restricted PEM to using only one public key method (RSA), one symmetric cipher (DES, in 3 "modes"), and two hash methods (MD2 and MD5). This made PEM consistent with the IETF's bias towards simplicity in implementation. That simplicity can foster faster validation of the methods by quickly getting independently developed software implementations into the hands of users. Arguably, it also minimizes the possibility of errors in implementations, thus giving greater assurance of security. Further, simple designs are easier to analyze for security problems.

It is interesting to note that even at this early date, the algorithm identifiers in PEM data headers were ASN.1 encoded.

The first implementation of PEM had only a single root key for the Internet Policy Registration Authority, and that key was built into the email client software so that all users could validate certificate chains starting from the root. Each user had a public key certificate; that certificate was attached to any signed message. Two users had to exchange signed email messages in order to learn each other's keys. Once they had done that, they could then send encrypted email. There was no central directory with public keys.

A major advocate for public key cryptography in the mid 1990's was the RSA corporation, the holder of the key patents for implementing the technology. They brought out a secure email product. The company at first worked with the IETF to define a standard for secure email, but then embarked on its own path to define the Public Key Cryptography Standards (PKCS). This left PEM in limbo.

From Out of Nowhere, Pretty Good Privacy (PGP)

In the meantime, political activist and software engineer Phil Zimmerman was one of many people frustrated by the slow pace of email security technology. Zimmerman wanted to facilitate encrypted email, and he wanted to show that it was not rocket science. In the late 1980's, he took the bull by the horns and wrote his own email security application. Taking a dig at the high assurance requirements of the IETF and the PKI requirements, he named his system Pretty Good Privacy. PGP was not derived from the PEM specifications or the X.400 precursors—it was Zimmerman's own design and implementation.

PGP was announced via a USENET group, and once it came onto the scene it become the common man's privacy solution. Although Zimmerman said that it was "an educational tool", it was fully functional open source software that could be used immediately. PEM, on the other hand, was used at only two companies, and there were no plans to commercialize it.

PGP had one major simplification over PEM that was a key point in rapid adoption. The PGP software protected messages with encryption and modification detection, but in a major departure from the IETF standards, it did not use certificates to represent public keys, and it did not use a hierarchy of trust. Zimmerman's simplifying idea was that users could develop trust in public keys through what we today call "social networking" and forgo the complication of certificate authorities and certificate hierarchies. In another departure from the IETF's philosophy of authentication, Zimmerman took pains to make the point that the trust was placed in the key itself, not any external notion of "identity". Pseudonyms for anonymous communication were an explicit goal of PGP.

PGP users could generate a public key immediately from the software distribution and begin using it. The public keys were represented in a simple block of data that could be sent in an email message to another user. Zimmerman encouraged people to put their keys on public servers established for that purpose, and MIT helped out by providing one. Although the system had seemed to have no authentication assurances, it provided a way to create a "web of trust". People could create ad hoc certificates just by signing someone else's key. If Alice convinced Bob that her public key was really one that she controlled, then he could sign her key and put that signed information onto a public server. Carol and Dave might do the same for Alice's key. Then if Ethan were looking for Alice's key, he might see that Carol's key had signed it. If Ethan already trusted Carol and her key, then Carol's signature on Alice's key might convince Ethan to trust Alice's key. Thus the web of trust (which coincided temporally with the "world wide web") began to grow.

One point of contention between PEM and PGP was the privacy of the user's identities. One of Zimmerman's design tenets was to avoid adding any unnecessary information about the email addresses or names of the correspondents in the secured part of the message. Although the unprotected Internet email headers give a lot of information about those identities, Zimmerman wanted to make sure that PGP separated the notions of Internet email identity from PGP identities and keys. If Bob wanted to use his oddly named email account "alice@example.com" to receive PGP email protected by a key for "bob@example.com", that was fine, and the PGP sending software would not put "bob@example.com" into any unencrypted part of the email.

Having produced PGP as his "proof of concept" for email privacy, Zimmerman felt that his software code base was sufficient for widespread adoption, and he was not interested in producing an IETF standards document. Nonetheless, he was no enemy of the IETF, and he urged the PEM designers to adopt some of his most important design principles. As he presciently wrote in 1991 on the PEM Development mailing list, urging developers to avoid adding unnecessary identifying information into the plaintext parts of messages:

> One of the many reasons PEM is such a useful contribution to the body
> politic is that without it, the Government can routinely scan the
> burgeoning flow of email traffic, with far less human effort and far
> less visibility than they could do with paper mail. With traffic
> analysis alone, surveillance of political activists and who they
> associate with can yield useful political intelligence.

During the next several years, PGP became very popular around the world, especially because of Zimmerman's defiance of pressure from the US government to restrict distribution of his software.

The four PEM specifications were final in 1993, but by then PGP was fast becoming the de facto standard for Internet email. At the same time, the IETF's specifications for email messages had changed to allow complex documents to be transmitted, and PEM needed to align itself with the new world of MIME. Complicating things even more was a rift in the The RSA Corporation had been an active participant in the PEM design group through their employee Burt Kalisky, they were about to separate from the IETF and pursue secure email standards through a different industry consortium.

Privacy Enhanced Mail (PEM), Part II: The Tangled Tale of Standardization

PEM did not specify any particular cryptographic methods, but the naming scheme had identifiers for DES, RSA, and MD2 and MD5 as their only examples of symmetric encryption, public key encrypt/signing, and hashing, respectively. The PEM architecture constituted the first definition of a complete, secure email system. As with any pioneer, it encountered numerous problems. The full solution to secure email standardization would not come for several years after the PEM specifications were complete, but the PEM experience was invaluable for motivating the work.

There were two kinds of signing, one that left the text of the message untouched and readable without special software, another that required PEM software to decode it. This allowed people to send signed email to non-PEM users without worrying about whether or not they had PEM software installed. A side effect of the transmission was to transmit the public key certificate to the recipient, thus boot-strapping secure communication.

PEM also supported sending encrypted email to multiple recipients. Each reci-pient got an encrypted copy of the symmetric encryption key in the encoded message structure.

The information about who was sending the message, and who it was destined for is information carried in ordinary email headers, but with public key technology, the name is not as important as the key. PEM had its own internal headers that defined the "IDs" of the sender and receivers. Those IDs could be public key identifiers or email names.

PEM was designed to work seamlessly over existing email services, so it needed a way to encode binary data, like signatures or encrypted data, into the ascii character set that Internet email used. The binary data used octets (or bytes) of 8 bits each, but the ascii character set used fewer than half of the 256 possible octet values. The encoding scheme that was chosen was a "3-to-4" map that would take 3 binary octets (24 bits), break them into 4 groups of six bits each, and then map each six bit quantity to a unique ascii character. Long before PEM, a similar method was employed in the Unix utility "uuencode". This is a form of radix-64 encoding, and PEM's variant on it, named "base64", turned out to be a lasting legacy of PEM, though all other details have faded away. Yet PEM was important as the motivator for much needed revisions to what would become known as Public Key Infrastructure (PKI).

Users of PEM needed to let their correspondents know about their public keys, and for this purpose PEM used public key certificates as defined in the ITU-T specification X.509. In these early days of public key technology, the PEM designers envisioned only one hierarchy with a single authority at the root—the Internet Policy Registration Authority(IPRA). The second level authorities would reflect different "policies", such as a state government that certified state agencies and cities, or a business directory service that certified non-profit corporations, or an entity that specified acceptable personal identifications (driver's licenses or pass-ports, etc.) for "persona" identificaton. The certificate authorities were at the third level and below, down to the individual users. Further, the X.509 system for names of certificate authorities assumed a parallel hierarchy (e.g. california.fresno. department-publicworks.northwest-office). As various organizations tried to adopt PEM, the strict rules for certificates became a major impediment. In the real world, businesses merge, government agencies split and reorganized, and names change.

PEM had a second specification entirely devoted to key management. RFC1422 covered a PEM message type for a "Certificate Revocation List" (CRL). These were intended to be a stopgap measure until widespread adoption of the X.509 services occurred. In the meantime, PEM's CRL message was a simple and reliable method for distributing the CRLs to end-users.

X.509 certificates were too difficult to use for large PEM deployments. The second level authorities' policies were difficult to learn or explain, the naming scheme was unwieldy, CA certificates had no syntactic distinguisher from end user certificates, the revocation scheme did not scale, and the top-down signing scheme had policy and management implications that needed to be addressed by putting more information into the certificates. Administrators found that they needed more information about certificate authorities in order to understand if they were trust-worthy. The hierarchy sometimes needed to be shortened by allowing a CA in one branch of a hierarchy to sign the certificate for a CA in a different branch. After a brief attempt to fix things by adding two new fields and calling it "X.509 version 2", the standardization groups retrenched. By 1998 they had developed a major rework of certificates with more fields, more flexible naming, formal definitions of CRLs, cross-signing, and a flexible system for adding new fields through formal extension fields. The X.509 version 3 certificate has proved an enduring legacy of the PEM experience.

One interesting point about X.509v3 today is that it is a standard defined by the ITU-T but separately defined by the IETF. The IETF defines the requirements for certificates used on the Internet for such things as email, secure communication channels, and website security, but these are consistent with the more general ITU-T definition. Nonetheless, in the interests of stability, the IETF publishes its own complete definition of Internet certificates. One standard, two heads!

PEM and MIME

But no sooner had the specs been finished than the task force discovered that they had a problem. While they had been working on secure email, other groups in the IETF had been defining a more general way of sending complex data. People needed to send photos, audio data, and even video, and the IETF had defined a way to send arbitrary data, even disparate kinds of data, in a single email message. This was the MIME standard, and it is what enables today's email attachments.

Encryption turns meaningful data into meaningless data, and that data is not something that humans can read. Email is geared towards a small character set, and the Internet email protocol, RFC822 and its successors, cannot transmit binary data. From this it follows that the data must be encoded into a smaller character set. PEM had solved this problem with "base64" encoding that packed 3 bytes of binary data in 4 bytes of ascii data. Yet this brought up another problem—how would the email handler for the recipient know that the message was encrypted? Email had already faced similar problems, and the usual solution was to add some extra information to the beginning of email. A line might be as simple as:

```
-----BEGIN PRIVACY-ENHANCED MESSAGE-----
```

Though this seemed logical, it ran into a variety of problems. Email software sometimes tried to be helpful and slightly adjust details of the message formatting, add ing or deleting a whitespace character here or there, and changing the character to indicate end of line, etc. This did not usually change the readability of normal email, but it played havoc with encrypted email and signed email. Cryptographic techniques would not work unless it could rely on software built to standards that guaranteed that headers could not be added and removed willy-nilly.

Encrypted email is not the only kind of binary data that people exchange, and a different part of the IETF had been working on this problem in the context of multimedia data. The MIME extensions to email were far along, and PEM was out of step with MIME conventions. In fact, MIME is what makes email attachments possible. We can send photos, music, compressed files, complex documents, and all manner of data in email attachments, and we expect it to work without a glitch. What the PEM group faced was the fact that all email clients would soon be supporting MIME, but they were not certain that they would support PEM, especially if its format was unrelated to MIME.

MIME Security Object Security Services (MOSS)

In 1994 the PEM working group decided that they needed to integrate their work with a major addition to Internet email, the Multipurpose Internet Mail Extension (MIME). MIME was becoming the accepted way to encode binary data files in email messages, but PEM's methods worked only for simple text messages. Moreover, a great benefit of MIME was that it could describe separate message parts within a single email message. As a result, MIME was an obvious and convenient mechanism for encoding "privacy enhancements". A marriage was in order.

Up until then, PEM used its own special markers to delineate secure email content:

```
-----BEGIN PRIVACY-ENHANCED MESSAGE-----
```

and

```
-----END PRIVACY-ENHANCED MESSAGE-----
```

with the expectation (or hope) that email software would not alter the content between the two markers. This simplistic method would not survive into the era of multipart messages with special encodings for binary contents.

A new IETF working group for PEM+MIME was formed, and it defined extensions to MIME for security enhancements based on PEM. This group defined the the standards for MIME Object Security Services (MOSS). MOSS used headers at the start of a message to announce that the message had internal MIME parts with security enhancements. Each security-enhanced MIME part was of either type "signed" or "encrypted". Each enhanced part had two subparts. One subpart was the cryptographic control information about either the signature or the encryption, and the other subpart was either the data to which the signature applied or the encrypted data. MOSS also addressed some of the aspects of key management by defining special MIME parts for requesting and sending public keys.

The MOSS designers sought to harmonize their work with a different secure email system, PGP. In doing so, they compromised on the tenet of PEM that mandated X.509 certificates and names. MOSS enlarged the identifier space to allow email names, the "distinguished name" in a certificate, or any arbitrary character string. This last form of ID opened the door to PGP key digests.

All in all, MOSS was a great improvement to PEM. Security enhancements could be extended to individual message parts using the MIME standards, which were already becoming popular. The victory was hollow, though, because by the time MOSS was published in 1995, it was already destined for the scrapheap.

During the time that the PEM was evolving to MOSS, the RSA corporation was working on its own version of secure email. Their interests were wider than the PEM working group's charter. RSA was interested in algorithm-independent coding of cryptographic parameters, secure representation of different kinds of public keys, extensions of X.509 certificates, certificate management, etc. They decided to work with an industry consortium instead of the IETF.

PKI, PKCS, and S/MIME

The whole subject of public keys, including all the representation and management utilities, comes under the umbrella term Public Key Infrastructure (PKI). Certificates are covered by the X.509 standard, and all the rest is covered by a group of standards that were originally called Public Key Cryptographic Standards (PKCS). They have a complicated history.

Apart from the indicators in an email message to denote that the message had encrypted content, there were a number of other issues that needed to be settled before certificiate-based email protections could reach the level of being well-defined and broadly useful. There were major issues to be dealt with concerning the definition and representation of a certificate, the meaning of terms within a certificate, the representation of keys, names, and signatures, requesting signatures for new certificates, dealing with keys that were unneeded or compromised, securely transferring private keys, etc. The standardization work on these issues bounced around among various groups before settling out into the current situation of cooperative bifurcation between the ITU-T and the IETF.

While the ITU-T remains the authority on X.509 certificates, Internet infrastructure providers rely on the IETF's X.509 version 3 specification. That specification is fully compatible with the ITU-T's definitions, but the IETF maintains its own documents that detail how certificates are represented and used for Internet purposes. The IETF documents also specifiy how Certificate Revocation Lists are represented.

The IETF has developed its own syntax for representing cryptographic data, CMS. That syntax is used for S/MIME data: key identifiers, algorithm identifiers, parameters, etc. The IETF also has its own format for bundling up keys for secure transfer.

The Public Key Cryptography Standards (PKCS) have a complicated history intertwined with many different organizations. PKCS started as an independent, non-IETF activity, just as the PEM and MOSS standards were being finalized. PKCS were supposed to define the cryptographic representations of data that are essential for interoperable secure email.

The responsibility for PKCS drifted between organizations for several years. During the 1990 s, the RSA corporation and the consortium that it aggregated developed the first set of PKCS specifications. These standards developed more detail and scope for the public key cryptography and data representations than the IETF groups had covered.

Over the years there have come to be 15 different parts to PKCS. Some of them were abandoned, some were brought to fruition, some continue to be developed. The original industry consortium left the work of completing the standards to the Open Systems Interconnection group within the CCITT (which became ITU-T). In 1995 the IETF, with cooperation from NIST, created the "Public Key Infrastructure X.509 (PKIX)" working group to develop refinements (profiles) of the ITU-T PKCS so that Internet services for email and website security and infrastructure security could be built on them. Moreover, the PKIX group saw the need to develop new services, particularly online services, for certificate management and Internet transport. Over time, the "profiles" became independent standards, usually compatible with the ITU-T, but not bound by them.

The PKCS#11 standard is currently under active development under the auspices of the OASIS consortium (https://www.oasis-open.org/).

A summary of PKCS parts (from the OASIS website):

- PKCS #1: mechanisms for encrypting and signing data using the RSA public key cryptosystem. This became the IETF's RFC 3447, issued in 2003.
- PKCS #3: a Diffie-Hellman key agreement protocol.
- PKCS #5: a method for encrypting a string with a secret key derived from a password. This became RFC 2898.
- PKCS #6: certificate extensions; phased out in favor of version 3 of X.509.
- PKCS #7: a general syntax for messages that include cryptographic enhancements such as digital signatures and encryption. This was absorbed into S/MIME and its multitude of documents.
- PKCS #8: a format for private key information. This became RFC 5208, a short description of the format for representing private keys and protected with symmetric encryption.
- PKCS #9: selected attribute types for use in the other PKCS standards. Published as an informational RFC (i.e., not part of other IETF standards).
- PKCS #10: syntax for certification requests. Published as an informational RFC (i.e., not part of other IETF standards).
- PKCS #11: a technology-independent programming interface, called Cryptoki, for cryptographic devices such as smart cards and PCMCIA cards. Currently under development by OASIS.
- PKCS #12: a portable format for storing or transporting a user's private keys, certificates, miscellaneous secrets, etc. In 2014, this standard was transferred from the RSA Corporation to the IETF, becoming RFC 7292. It builds on

PKCS#8 and greatly extends it. [The "p12" file format has been used for bundling key for transporting to email and web clients for some time.]

- PKCS #13: mechanisms for encrypting and signing data using Elliptic Curve Cryptography. Apparently abandoned.
- PKCS #14: pseudo-random number generation. Abandoned.
- PKCS #15: a complement to PKCS #11 giving a standard for the format of cryptographic credentials stored on cryptographic tokens. Standardized by the International Organization for Standardization as ISO/IEC 7816-15:2004

The PKCS#12 standard became the IETF's "Personal Information Exchange" standard for encoding and protecting public/private key pairs when they are moved from one device to another. PKCS#7 survives in the signature attachment filename "smime.p7 s". A few of the other PKCS sections live on as the basis for RFC's on specialized methods of working with hardware devices. The OASIS organization continues work on some of the PKCS subsections.

A certificate is, at its heart, simple to describe: a public key, the identity of the owner, the signer's key, and the signer's signature over those three crucial elements. Yet, the work of obtaining a stable definition has been spread over three decades. The PKIX group published "Internet X.509 Public Key Infrastructure Certificate and CRL Profile" in 1999. The final version was published in 2008. It turns out that using and managing certificates is fraught with complexity, and that complexity has become embodied in the certificate definition.

The original X.509 specification from the X.500 Directory Services specification covered the basic requirements for transmitting, identifying, and authenticating public keys within a certification hierarchy. As security administrators gained experience from trying to use the architecture for large numbers of users and with non-trivial hierarchy depths, they felt that it would be helpful to have more information to facilitate management functions.

A second version of X.509 added two more fields, but the response from administrators was that they needed still more. As the standardization groups worked to find consensus on a small number of fields, they came to realize that the diversity of opinions on how to establish the trustworthiness of certificiate issuer was going to rely on more fields. Some of those fields would be using data that might be unique to only a section of the hierarchy. Version 3 of the standard was forged to satisfy diverse needs by adding the "extension" capability, leaving the original fields as required, adding new fields, and allowing an unlimited number of new fields in the certificate extensions.

The Cryptographic Message Syntax, CMS

The syntax for representations of cryptographic messages was covered in the seventh of the PKCS series, and it was taken under the wing of yet another IETF working group—"networks". The CMS standard [15] is based on a formal definition of the syntax elements for representing algorithms, algorithm parameters, encrypted data, nonces, etc. That syntax and its representation in terms of bytes and bits became the basis for representing data in certificates and secure email attachments.

The things that go into cryptographic syntax are usually different for each algorithm. The following show how public keys are defined in CMS. The first data structure defines the generic data structure for a public key, and it has an identifier at the beginning signifying that it is an RSA public key type, there are optional parameters, and there is a bit that determines the purpose of the key. The second data structure defines the public key elements (the modulus and the exponent), and the third data structure defines the meaningful names of the usage bits.

```
pk-rsa-pss PUBLIC-KEY ::= {
    IDENTIFIER id-RSASSA-PSS
    KEY RSAPublicKey
    PARAMS TYPE RSASSA-PSS-params ARE optional
    CERT-KEY-USAGE { .... }
}

RSAPublicKey ::= SEQUENCE {
        modulus         INTEGER,    -- n
        publicExponent  INTEGER     -- e
}

KeyUsage ::= BIT STRING {
        digitalSignature        (0),
        nonRepudiation          (1), -- recent editions of X.509 have
                                -- renamed this bit to contentCommitment
        keyEncipherment         (2),
        dataEncipherment        (3),
        keyAgreement            (4),
        keyCertSign             (5),
        cRLSign                 (6),
        encipherOnly            (7),
        decipherOnly            (8) }
```

Whereas previous security standards had used their own conventions for representing the names of algorithms (e.g. "RSA" or "DES"), and their own methods for designating a symmetric key or a public key, CMS presented a uniform method for representing all things cryptographic. This meant that developers needed only one software library to read and write cryptographic information for use with any almost any IETF standard.

The underlying lexicographic representation of CMS elements is an abstract notation called ASN.1. ASN.1 describes numbers, strings, object identifiers, time, etc. The actual representation of ASN.1 in bytes is described by its oft maligned Binary Encoding Rules (BER). BER has several ways to represent numbers and strings, and even the same value can be represented in more than one way.

This thwarts the precision demanded by cryptographic algorithms. Therefore X.509 and CMS use a subset of BER call the Distinguished Encoding Representation (DER). A frequent complaint about BER/DER is that its binary data representation is complicated, and as a result, the CMS data structures cannot be parsed by casual examination of the byte strings.

S/MIME, Secure/Multipurpose Internet Mail Extensions

Another product of the PKCS industry working group was a set of extensions to the IETF MIME protocol. The extensions were simply a set of additional headers indicating that a message part had cryptographic enhancements. These could be encryption or signing or a certificate management function. The body of a protected MIME part was encoded in a format that was the subject of another PKCS work topic denoted as PKCS#7. In 1998, the consortium documented this work in an IETF document as "S/MIME version 2". The document is careful to note that it is not an IETF standard, but it has historic interest. The successor protocol, S/MIME version 3, became in IETF standard in 1998. This was a mere five years after MIME itself was published as a standard.

The IETF's S/MIME working group produced the standards that are the final word on adding certificate-based cryptography to MIME objects. The group needed to pick up from where PEM and MOSS had left off, extending their work with new MIME headers and adding a much more flexible cryptographic representation structure. The working group did a prodigious amount of work in achieving its purpose and extending it. Over its lifetime, the group produced 50 documents covering everything from using X.509v3 certificates to use of Identity-Based Encryption [4], and to avoidance of "small subgroup attacks."

It is important to note that MIME is used for more than just email, and S/MIME can be applied to any MIME object. HTTP can transfer MIME objects, and S/MIME headers are often useful on files that have been signed or encrypted.

Despite, or because of, its simplicity and resemblance to earlier ways of attaching security headers, S/MIME succeeded in becoming widely used. From its first version in 1999 until its most recent revision in 2010, it has kept up-to-date on cryptographic algorithms.

S/MIME defines one new MIME "media" type to indicate that there are security enhancements in the data that follows: application/pkcs7-mime. That media type can be followed by a parameter indicating that the data is encrypted: "smime-type = enveloped-data" or "smime-type = signed-data".

There is a second way to represent signed data, one that largely transparent to those who do not use secure email readers, making it the most commonly used security enhancement. This is the "detached signature" which fits into the MIME multipart scheme very nicely with the addition of the Content-Type value "multipart/signed":

```
Content-Type: multipart/signed;
    protocol="application/pkcs7-signature"; micalg=sha1
```

In the example above, the MIME part precedes two subparts, one with the message content, which can be any kind of MIME part, and the second with the smime-type of "signed-data".

Most people who receive these multipart signed messages are only aware of the signature part because it appears as an attachment with the filename "smime.p7s". The S/MIME signature on the message is encoded in that attachment, as are the sender's certificates.

The signature hash algorithm, in the example above, is the "micalg" (message integrity algorithm) SHA1. It may seem strange to see the algorithm mentioned in the header, but implementors like to have it revealed before they do any further cryptographic processing. They can apply the algorithm to the preceding MIME part immediately, and then the hash value is ready to compare against whatever is encoded in the signature.

The reader might wonder, where's the cryptography? After all, the headers are merely signals that cryptography is happening somewhere, but where are the details? All the cryptographic details about algorithms and lengths and sizes are in the data following the S/MIME headers, encoded in the Crypographic Message Syntax. S/MIME adds a few data types of its own to CMS, and those, in combination with the additional MIME types, constitute S/MIME.

The file extensions in S/MIME headers are a holdover from the original PKCS specifications, and they serve an advisory role today, because the CMS payload supercedes its function. The "p7s" extension indicates a signature, "p7m" is enveloped data (signed and/or encrypted), "p7z" is compressed data, and "p7c" means that certificates are the only payload.

In earlier versions of S/MIME, there was some support for certificate management, but today's S/MIME leaves most of the work to the protocols designed specifically for that purpose by the PKIX working group. S/MIME does carry certificates as part of a signed message, encoded in the CMS data that is the signature. This supports the "exchange signed messages once; encrypt thereafter" model of person-to-person certificate bootstrapping.

Two IETF Request for Comments (RFC) make up S/MIME version 2: RFC 2311 (http://www.ietf.org/rfc/rfc2311.txt), which established the standard for messages, and RFC 2312 (http://www.ietf.org/rfc/rfc2312.txt), which established the standard for certificate handling. Together, these RFCs provided the first Internet standards-based framework that vendors could follow to deliver interoperable message security solutions.

After all the different attempts to define security headers for email, it is strange that S/MIME is not completely transparent. The answer to the question of "what is an S/MIME message" is best answered from one of its defining documents [26]:

```
Because S/MIME takes into account interoperation in non-MIME
environments, several different mechanisms are employed to carry the
type information, and it becomes a bit difficult to identify S/MIME
messages.  The following table lists criteria for determining whether
or not a message is an S/MIME message.  A message is considered an
S/MIME message if it matches any of the criteria listed below.

The file suffix in the table below comes from the "name" parameter in
the Content-Type header field, or the "filename" parameter on the
Content-Disposition header field.  These parameters that give the
file suffix are not listed below as part of the parameter section.

Media type:  application/pkcs7-mime
parameters:  any
file suffix: any

Media type:  multipart/signed
parameters:  protocol="application/pkcs7-signature"
file suffix: any

Media type:  application/octet-stream
parameters:  any
file suffix: p7m, p7s, p7c, p7z
```

An example of a message encrypted and encoded as an S/MIME message (from RFC 5751):

```
Content-Type: application/pkcs7-mime; smime-type=enveloped-data;
      name=smime.p7m
Content-Transfer-Encoding: base64
Content-Disposition: attachment; filename=smime.p7m

rfvbnj756tbBghyHhHUujhJhjH77n8HHGT9HG4VQpfyF467GhIGfHfYT6
7n8HHGghyHhHUujhJh4VQpfyF467GhIGfHfYGTrfvbnjT6jH7756tbB9H
f8HHGTrfvhJhjH776tbB9HG4VQbnj7567GhIGfHfYT6ghyHhHUujpfyF4
0GhIGfHfQbnj756YT64V
```

Understanding S/MIME in enough detail to implement it means conquering ASN.1, DER, CMS, X.509v3 certificates, base64 encoding, RSA and DSA public key algorithms and their key encodings, the representation of a public key signature, the SHA1 and SHA2 hash algorithms, the AES symmetric cipher and its encoding, the 3DES symmetric cipher and its encoding, representing the public key encryption of a symmetric cipher key, and the S/MIME headers for email.

OpenPGP: PGP as an IETF Standard

A completely independent concept for secure email took a more direct line from initial concept to its embodiment today as an IETF standard with open source and commercial implementations.

As noted previously, PGP gained immediate popularity, and Zimmerman spoke out as an advocate of privacy technology for the masses. In 1994, with the help of an international team of collaborators, PGP 2.0 hit the streets, and Zimmerman found himself embroiled in legal issues arising from the US government's export limits on cryptography and patent infringement claims related to his use of the RSA public key algorithm. As Zimmerman worked with a team of lawyers to resolve these problems, PGP gained traction as the solution to the private communication needs of Internet users.

PGP 3.0 came out in 1996, and it was a major rework of the system. It added ciphers that avoided patent issues, and it was designed as a software library for developers instead of being simply an "app".

Shortly afterward, the IETF undertook the task of standardizing PGP. The PGP team felt this was necessary to ensure that PGP could be both a commercial product and a freely available application. The IETF working group used "OpenPGP" as their name for the encrypted email system. In sharp contrast to the S/MIME and PKIX documents, OpenPGP is a compact and complete specification for encrypted email.

- RFC 1991 PGP Message Exchange Formats, August 1996. This documented the PGP 2.x implementations that were by then in use around the world.
- RFC 2015 MIME Security with Pretty Good Privacy (PGP), October 1996. The MIME headers for PGP messages were defined here, much as PEM had done with MOSS. It was a simple scheme that allowed PGP to be easily encapsulated with headers indicating encryption or signature or key content.
- RFC 2440 OpenPGP Message Format (obsolete), November 1998. This documented the design of the PGP 3.0 system (aka PGP 5.0).
- RFC 3156 MIME Security with OpenPGP, August 2001. This defines the same MIME headers as in RFC 2015, but it extends them with parameters for more algorithms than PGP supported in the 1990 s.
- RFC 4880 OpenPGP Message Format, November 2007. This replaced RFC 2440; the changes were largely editorial and did not affect interoperability. The doubling of the RFC number from the 1998 version is an amusing footnote on PGP's standardization.

PGP never saw the need for S/MIME. Instead, the designers opted for a scheme more akin to the PEM MOSS headers. The MIME encoding for OpenPGP is simple. An encrypted message has this information in the email message header:

```
Content-Type: multipart/encrypted; boundary=xxx;
    protocol="application/pgp-encrypted"
```

The message will have two internal MIME parts. One simply repeats the encryption information:

```
Content-Type: application/pgp-encrypted
```

and the other has the encrypted, encoded data with a header for arbitrary encoded data followed by PGP's internal header:

```
Content-Type: application/octet-stream

-----BEGIN PGP MESSAGE-----

    ...
```

A signed message is equally simple. The main message header signals the signature data, and names the algorithm that assures data integrity:

```
Content-Type: multipart/signed; boundary=yyy; micalg=pgp-md5;
protocol="application/pgp-signature"
```

The signed message has two MIME parts, one with the actual message, and a second part with the PGP signature preceded by the header:

```
Content-Type: application/pgp-signature
```

A third header type signals that a PGP key block follows:

```
Content-Type: application/pgp-keys
```

PGP, like PEM and S/MIME, uses radix-64 encoding to turn binary data into ascii characters that the email transfer protocol can deal with. PGP uses a slightly different character set and calls the result "ascii armor" (asc). PGP's internal "PGP MESSAGE" delimiters enclose ascii armored data.

The choice of supported ciphers for PGP has always included more variety than the IETF embraced. In its early days, PGP favored ciphers developed outside the United States. OpenPGP today recognizes Blowfish, Twofish, CAST5, AES, and 3DES as symmetric ciphers. The Camellia cipher was added in 2004.

OpenPGP recognizes RSA, ElGamal, and DSA as its public key methods. In 2012 the definitions for elliptic curve cryptography were added. The PGP implementation in the GNU Privacy Guard (GPG) software supports elliptic curves as of release 2.1.

The number of pages of standards devoted to describing OpenPGP is far less than that devoted to S/MIME. The two systems had radically different evolutions from concept to running code, but they are really nothing more than two variants of the same core idea: public key cryptography protecting the secrecy of symmetric cipher keys, and encrypted data embedded in Internet email.

Chapter 3
How Does Secure Email Work?

Public keys make it easy to keep email private:

- The sender:
    - Finds the public key for the recipient.
    - Encrypts the message.
    - Sends the message.
- The recipient decrypts the message.

    Assuring authenticity of the sender is just as easy:

- The sender signs and sends the message.
- The recipient:

    - Gets the public key for the sender.
    - Verifies the signature on the message.

Most email clients today can be configured so that the steps are automatic and nearly invisible. The problems arise when trying to get a key for the first time, when trying to find a key for a new recipient, or when trying to convince a new correspondent to get a key for PGP or S/MIME.

The software that implements the email security algorithms does a great deal of work behind the scenes for the sender. The sender has to make some subjective decisions about which keys to trust and to use for first-time correspondents:

- User action: If the recipient's public key is not already in your contacts list, find it (by asking for it, searching for it on websites, etc.). If you have not already made a decision about the trustworthiness of the key, do that now. For S/MIME, examine the certificate chain; for PGP, look at the key signers and the "web of trust".
- User action: If you are going to sign the message, select your signing key.
- Compute the digest of the message. For S/MIME, use an algorithm that is secure and supported by the recipient. PGP only uses one digest method, SHA1.
- Select a symmetric cipher for encrypting the message. Use an algorithm that is secure and supported by your recipient.

© The Author(s) 2015
H. Orman, *Encrypted Email*,
SpringerBriefs in Computer Science,
DOI 10.1007/978-3-319-21344-6_3

- Using a good source of randomness, select a random key for the symmetric cipher.
- Encrypt the message and the digest using the symmetric cipher and the random key
- Using the recipient's public key algorithm and public key, encrypt the random key.
- If signing the message, use your private key to sign the message digest.
- Optional: include your public key certificate chain in the message. If using PGP, you can include your key block.
- Encode the encrypted message, the encrypted key, your signature on the digest (optional), and some identifying information about the recipient's key and your signing key (optional) into a standardized message format (CMS with BER or DER for S/MIME, or PGP packets).
- Encode formatted message information into an ascii character set using a standard method (PEM—aka base64—for S/MIME, armored ascii for PGP).
- Add the appropriate S/MIME or MIME/PGP headers.
- Send the message over the Internet.

The recipient's actions are the reverse of the above. Signed messages will be verified automatically, even if the user has not made a decision about the trustworthiness of the sender's key. Encrypted email will be decrypted automatically and checked for modification. Any new keys included in the message will be added to your key chain but without any trust indication.

Altogether, an email system does quite a lot of work to deal with secure email. There are the two important security properties that make it all worthwhile. The first is that only a person who knows the private key can ever read the message or even deduce anything about the contents. A second essential property is that the decrypted message is either exactly the one that the sender composed, or else the recipient can tell that it has been altered. This latter property is guaranteed through a signature over the message. The encryption methods use modification detection codes for this purpose, and they are very good but not mathematically guaranteed if the message is only encrypted.

A third property is often desirable, but it is not universally sought. This property is a "proof" that the message came from the person purporting to send it. More specifically, the message is cryptographically associated with a public key, and only someone who know the private key could have composed the message. There are two possible drawbacks to this kind of strong authentication of the sender. One is that it might be possible for an eavesdropper to make a guess about the signer's key, and depending on the exact details of the representation of the encrypted message, he might be able to verify his guess. This would cut into the privacy of the sender, to some degree. The email headers do reveal something about the sender, though not about his public key.

Even if the signature is hidden by encryption, there is yet another privacy issue: some people do not want permanent attribution of their messages. The recipient can decrypt a message and show it to a third party, revealing the attribution. Therefore, "encryption only" methods include no digital signature, and they leave the attribution of origin to be determined by the recipient's subjective evaluation of the message contents and the context of the conversation (Fig. 3.1).

Although it is easy to describe the process of sending and receiving secure email, there is a tremendous amount of work that goes on under the hood, and there are many things that can go awry. The recipient might find that the message cannot be decrypted. One party or the other will have to change something—a key, the encoding method, the way attachments are handled. The totality of those choices determines how much trust to put into the communication.

To get a deeper understanding of some of the complications it is necessary to understand a little more about public key algorithms. Messages are encrypted using public key and symmetric algorithms because the public key system by itself is not a practical solution for encryption. Public key methods require a great deal of arithmetic to encrypt a small amount of data.

Assume that k represents a short message, and we have some way to turn that short message into data that can only be read by one particular user who has published the public values e and N. Then the RSA equation looks simple:

$$E = \text{encrypt}(k) = k^e \bmod N$$

which means to multiply k times k times k ..., until k has been used e times, then take the remainder of dividing this by N. In this scheme, N is an extremely large

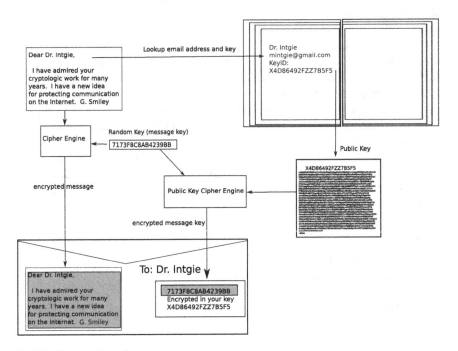

Fig. 3.1 Encrypted email

number, hundreds of decimal digits. Each secure email user constructs his own number N. As a result, this simple equation can keep a computer fully occupied with the arithmetic while encrypting only a short message. Long messages or large files cannot be encrypted this way because it would run into hours of work. This is the price of public key cryptography. Fortunately, the price only has to be paid for one small piece of data.

It turns out that decryption is almost exactly the same as encryption, except that it uses a secret number d known only to the owner of the number N. The trick to this is to make N the product of two large, secret prime numbers, P and Q. For any e, there is a corresponding number d that can "undo" the equation shown above by the very similar operation:

$$k = \text{decrypt}(E) = E^d \bmod N$$

For anyone who knows N but does not know what P and Q are, it is extremely difficult to calculate that all-important number d. But, for the person who chose P and Q and keeps them secret, d is easy to calculate because it is the inverse of e $\bmod$ $(P - 1)(Q - 1)$, which is to say

$$e * d = 1 \bmod (P - 1)(Q - 1)$$

For the public key owner who knows P and Q, the calculation of a modular inverse can be done quickly, even when the modulus has thousands of bits. The calculation only has to be done once, when the public key is first created using the large primes P and Q.

The whole message is not encrypted using a public key method. Instead, it is encrypted using a symmetric cipher designed to be very fast on today's computers. The key for the symmetric cipher is a randomly chosen number, typically from 128 to 256 bits. In the equations shown above, the number k is the symmetric cipher key. The public key method encrypts the key for the symmetric cipher, and the symmetric cipher encrypts the message. The recipient decrypts the symmetric key and then decrypts the entire message.

Suppose that Alice wants to send an encrypted message to Bob. Her message is an object that consists of a string of bytes, say a file or text string. Let's denote the whole thing by m. If Bob has told Alice that he uses the number N and the exponent e as his public key parameters, then they can communicate using the RSA public key method and the AES symmetric cipher as follows:

Alice:

1. Choose a random 16-byte key k for the symmetric cipher.
2. $\text{encrypt}_{(N,e)}(k) = k^e \bmod N = E(k)$
   $\text{symmetric-encrypt}(k, m) = \text{AES-encrypt}_k(m) = E'(m)$
3. Send $\{E(k), E'(m)\}$ to Bob

Bob:

1. $k = (E(k))^d \bmod N$
2. message = AES-decrypt$_k$(E'(m))

As noted earlier, the two numbers e and N together are called an RSA public key. There are other public key systems, and they usually have at least two parameters per key.

The public key parts of the computation are relatively slow—thousands of times slower than the symmetric cipher computation for a small amount of data. Fortunately, the public key operations are done only on a small piece of data, 32 bytes or fewer for the symmetric key k. The symmetric cipher can encrypt larger messages, with attachments, in the same amount of time.

At the dawn of the modern cryptography era for the Internet, there were only a few symmetric key ciphers to choose from. The cipher most commonly used was the DES standard. From its inception, there was skepticism from security experts about its security [7], particularly its key length, which was only 56 bits. Today there are many excellent symmetric key ciphers to choose from, with key lengths to suit even the most paranoid users.

What About Authentication?

As we mentioned before, public keys have a second application that is as important as encryption. They can also authenticate the sender of a message. In a secure email system, users typically have two public keys: one for signing outgoing messages and one for receiving encrypted messages. One of the keys, usually the signing key, is the primary identifying key for the user.

If Alice publishes her public key for verifying her signature, V_{Alice}, and a message M, she can create a signature for the message using her private signing key, S_{Alice} by signing a "summary" of M that is much shorter than the whole message. Just as with public key encryption, signing every block of M would take too much time, but signing a summary that is about 20 bytes long requires an acceptably small amount of time.

The function that produces a message summary is called a "hash function" or a "modification detection code". People have been worrying about text modification for millennia. Ancient scribes had to copy texts verbatim as they tried to preserve and promulgate human knowledge, and they often made mistakes. They devised various ways to check their work, and some of the methods involved arithmetic. By assigning a numeric value to each alphabetic character, a scribe could add up the values for a line of text in the original. The value in the copy should match exactly, and if it didn't, the scribe could go back and look for the error.

Today we have many options for hash functions that serve the same purpose. The functions take a message of any length and turn it into a short string of bytes quickly—more quickly than enciphering it, for example. However, the function must be one that is very unlikely to produce the same value for two different messages (a "collision"). Moreover, it should be infeasible to take one message and produce another with the same summary value.

If H is a function meeting those restrictions, then Alice can sign her message in the following way. She publishes her public key parameters using a certificate or PGP key block. Let's call the parameters P_{Alice}. Along with those she publishes the name of the hash function H. Then she proceeds with the following computation:

$$\text{Signature of Alice on message } M = \text{Sig}_{Alice}(H(M)) = S_{Alice}(M)$$

Anyone can verify the signature by using Alice's public verification key parameters in P_{Alice} on the message M by computing the function H(M) and checking that the following equality is true:

$$V_{Alice}(S_{Alice}(M)) = H(M)$$

Alice's signature can be sent along with the message M as an attachment or as a clearly delineated message extension. It is important that the recipient receives exactly the same message that Alice sent—no changes to the line lengths, no insertions of extra spaces or blank lines, etc.

Because anyone can verify a signature, if Alice does not want anyone but Bob to know that she sent the message, she will need to hide her signature. That can be done if Alice encrypts the message using Bob's public key P_{Bob} and her signature:

$$\text{Encrypt}_{P_{Bob}}(M, \text{Sig}_{Alice}(H(M)))$$

When Bob receives and decrypts the message, he will have both M and $S(H(M))$, and he can use Alice's public verification key for originator authentication.

Another method of computing the message summary allows Alice to sign the encrypted message without giving up signature privacy. If the symmetric key k is included as part of the message summary calculation, then Alice can send four items to Bob:

$$E_{P_{Bob}}(k), E_k(M), H(E_k(M)|k), \text{Sig}_{Alice}(H(E_k(M)|k))$$

The symbol "|" means the concatenation of two bitstrings.

Upon receipt, Bob can decrypt the symmetric key k, compute the hash function of the encrypted message concatenated with the key k, verify that Alice signed the encrypted text, and then decrypt the message M. An observer can see the signature, but he does not know what value was signed because he does not know k. This method preserves Alice's privacy even if someone is recording all the encrypted email on Bob's server.

How Certificates Work

The central problem in secure email, or for any Internet security, is "why should I believe that the public key really belongs to the person I think it does"? Certificates are one way of answering the question. A certificate answers the question by saying "someone I trust says so." This works under the assumption that there is a hierarchy of trust among certificate signers.

An email certificate is a representation of a person's name, email address, and public key (or keys), and the signature of some certificate authority (CA) on the hash of that information. If the certificate is for "Alice T. Smith", why should you believe that it has her correct public key? In a purely logical sense, it is because the certificate authority is assumed to be trustworthy, and thus, its signature on Alice's data is trustworthy. Why is the certificate authority trustworthy? It inherits trust from the signature of a higher level certificate authority that attests to the authenticity of key of the lower-level CA. And why is the higher-level CA trustworthy? Because ultimately, there is a "root certificate authority" that signed the certificate for a CA in this chain of certificates. The root certificate authorities are assumed to be as trustworthy as can be humanly achieved (Fig. 3.2).

The root CAs are supposed to be well-known government or business entities that carry out due diligence before signing the certificates for other CAs. Their certificates are signed by themselves (self-signed), and those certificates are widely available on the Internet. Your browser comes configured with a list of a few dozen root CAs that are trusted to sign certificates for other CAs. OpenSSL comes configured with a similar list. You can add or delete root CAs in your configuration, though this should be done with caution. Sometimes adding a root CA violates the

Fig. 3.2 Certificate concept

security policy set for the computer; in that case system administrator privileges will be required.

Are root CAs totally trustworthy? For the most part, yes, but they cannot be omniscient, and their service cannot detect all forms of fraud. Even the most careful notary cannot absolutely validate every document, and at its heart, the system depends on human judgments. Thus, a certificate is only one form of authentication, good for most purposes, but not likely good enough for very high risk transactions unless you have other reasons to trust the CA.

Let us suppose that you receive Alice's certificate, signed by her organizational CA. Is this enough for you to trust Alice? In the world of Public Key Infrastructure (PKI), you must verify the signature of the CA that signed her certificate. In our illustration, this is her "Organizational Unit CA" (a fictionalized generic name). Should you trust that signature? That trust is established by verifying the signature of the "Organization's CA" on the certificate for the "Organizational Unit CA". This proceeds up the chain until you reach the "Root CA" and its self-signed certificate.

The PKI world assumes that you see the certificates for root CA's fairly often, and you do not need to verify their signature every time. Further, you probably see the "Secondary CA" and "Intermediate CA" often, and you only need to verify that signature chain once a day or once a week; in the meantime, you can keep their certificates and signatures cached. Furthermore, once you have verified Alice's certificate, you don't need to repeat this until you reverify one of the CAs above her certificate (Fig. 3.3).

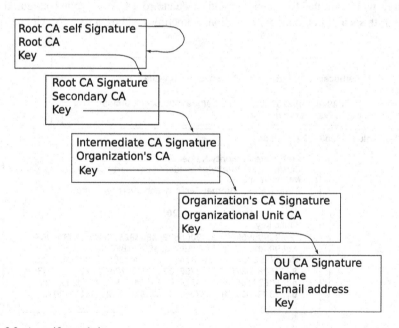

Fig. 3.3 A certificate chain

Why does an organization become a root CA? How can it take on the work of trying to validate the credentials of someone who purports to be the Chief Security Office for Example.com Corporation? The business case for root CAs requires that they charge for their services: certificate issuance, handling maintenance requests, etc. The certificates can be bundled with other services, such as email or website hosting or cloud services. Of course, it is not necessary for every certificate to be signed by a root CA, and you can avoid paying for a certificate by requesting that some other entity issue your certificate; that, plus the certificate chain for the signer, will let anyone validate your key. But, there are not very many entities that will do this except for their own employees.

Although the certificate hierarchy is by far the most common structure for certificates, it is possible to construct any kind of graph through "cross-certification". A cross-certificate has a CA as the subject, and the signer is a CA that belongs to a different root CA. The cross signing creates a trust relationship between two independent trust hierarchies. This can be useful if two organizations have become partners but have used different root CAs, for example. The drawback to the scheme is that it can greatly complicate the process of finding a certificate chain that can be validated back to a trusted root. While the technique has obvious utility, it is not universally supported.

Certificates do not last forever. They expire or are revoked. The expiration time is evident from the certificate, but revocation can happen at any time that the key holder decides it is necessary. The motivation might be that the organization's new security officer thinks that the keys should be longer, or perhaps the organization has a new structure and wants to reissue keys that reflect the new structure. If malware has been a problem, an organization might want to protect themselves against compromise of their secret key by switching to a new one. In any case, correspondents with the organization need to go to extra work to discover revocations. The list of revoked keys is called a CRL, and it published by the CA. Correspondents must go to the CA's publication site to retrieve the list and process it.

There are other problems that surround using PKI. Suppose you find that a CA certificate that is in your cache has expired. The usual interpretation of PKI policy requires that you now stop trusting any of the certificates that it has signed, of course. In some systems this is interpreted more strictly, and any certificates that *would expire* after the CA expiry time are considered untrusted. For this reason, CAs usually issue new certificates long before any of their signed certificates would expire. A CA can its currently valid key to sign a new certificate with a later expiration date. The new certificate can be accepted as a valid alternative to the older one, and it can be used to sign new certificates for the CA's clients. When the CAs original key expires, the older certificate can be discarded in favor the newer one. The overlap of validity periods assures continuity of credentials for authentication.

Not everyone does this in a timely manner, and it is all too common to get warnings about expired website certificates! Renewing a certificate seems to be about as much fun as paying taxes.

The problem with CRLs is that they are not easy to check. They are published and signed by CAs, but how do you request revocation, how do you validate your request? Where do you find a CRL, how often do you check it, what are the consequences of revoking a key if there is no replacement? These are among the many questions that complicate PKI management.

How PGP Trust Works

PGP is deliberately built on a different notion of trust than the Public Key Infrastructure of hierarchical certificates. Phil Zimmerman did not want to have a set of pre-designated authorities control the creation of signed keys. Instead, he wanted a system in which individuals could make their own decisions about which keys were trustworthy. His idea was radical at the time, but it seems much more natural in today's environment of social networks. PGP is based on a "web of trust" instead of a "chain of trust".

A web of trust is built "bottom up". A person can create a public/private key pair and publish the public key along with his name and email address. In the PKI world, he would need to have a certificate authority sign this key, but in the web of trust, people send their public keys to one another in email messages, they can endorse other people's keys by signing them (acting as a "mini-CA"), and they publish keys and key signatures on public websites created just for that purpose. Individual users make their own trust decisions about keys based on the totality of information available to them.

PGP creates its "web of trust" by making trust transitive. An individual user Alice, for example, can publish the fact that she trusts a key for Bob by using her key to sign Bob's key. A key can accumulate more and more signatures. As more and more people trust Bob's key by signing it, people might be persuaded to use the key. The reasoning is "I know Alice and I believe that 'A' is her public key; Alice has used 'A' to say that she trust's Bob's key; I will take Alice's word for it and trust Bob's key." If Carol has signed Bob's key, someone who knows both Alice and Carol might find the fact that they both trust Bob's key to be particularly cogent.

PGP builds up a set of relationships among keys without using a central authority, without any infrastructure for requesting certificates or certificate signing. All you need to do is to create a key and let people know about it.

It is important to keep in mind that you can receive keys through signed email messages, and you can verify messages that are signed with them, without "trusting" the key. Even if the message is signed properly and the key seems to belong to the sender, the association need not be considered valid. The very ease of creating PGP keys means that they have little inherent trustworthiness. They only acquire value through the process of obtaining endorsing signatures. Therefore, before you use a PGP key for sending encrypted email to the owner, your key management software will want you to explicitly endorse it by signing it. You do not need to send your endorsement to anyone else, but your signature is the way you let the key management software know that you are willing to entrust confidential information to that encryption key.

When should you trust a key? The most common and simplest basis for trust is to receive it in an email message from someone you know well. You can call Bob on the phone and say "did you just send me your key, and is this the identifier for the key (FA73E1A94949C177)?" or you can meet in person and look at each other's computer screens to compare the key ID against Bob's keyring. The key identifier comes in two forms—the full "hash" value of the key, which will be somewhere between 16 and 32 bytes, or the truncated hash value that is the last 8 bytes.

The flexibility of PGP trust has not gained universal admiration. In 1999 a study [32] of usability factors showed that people needed a surprising amount of training to become familiar with and proficient at making PGP trust decisions. The same is true for many aspects of secure email usage.

Certificates Versus PGP Keys

In terms of features and software for key management, PGP and S/MIME do not have a great deal of difference in authentication capabilities for email. The main difference is that it is easy to specify why a certificate chain is trusted ("it goes back to a trusted root") but there is no single way of describing why a PGP key is trusted.

PGP keys have some analogies with X.509v3 certificates in that they are a binding between a public key and some information about a person's identity. On the other hand, PGP keys are much more agile and expressive than certificates. It is somewhat like the difference between a driver's license and a badge making machine. A certificate is meant to be an authoritative document about identity and a public key, but PGP users can use their keys to sign other keys, create more keys for themselves, and use more than one email address with a key.

There is little structure imposed on PGP key sets. The "primary keys" can vouch for ("sign") any number of subkeys, and it is easy to generate new primary keys and subkeys. PGP does not restrict the number of email addresses associated with keys, and it is possible for different users to share keys. This leaves open the possibility of establishing any number of end-user policies about accepting and using PGP keys. There are not many "policy engines" available for imposing rules on the process. One could, for example, have a policy that designated a set of PGP keys as "trusted authorities", and any key signed by a trusted authority would be automatically trusted. This could result in a policy very similar to the hierarchy of X.509 certificates.

An X.509 certificate binds a key to an identity, and only the certificate authority that issued the certificate can modify the information. PGP, on the other hand, allows a key to sign additional information related to the user, such extra email addresses. Whereas X.509v3 expects the "subject identifier" character string to be used to look up information about the user, PGP relies on the public key itself to identify information about the user. PGP lets a primary key act analogously to a certificate authority. The primary key can sign other keys (subkeys) for the same user, and the subkeys can sign additional information about the user—identifying information, preferences for symmetric ciphers, and other arbitrary data. The collection of information is like a bundle of small certificates, each one with a specific nugget of information and signed by a user key. Furthermore, the primary key can sign information about keys belonging to other people, and this signing ability creates the web of trust. X.509 systems normally do not authorize end users to issue their own certificates, but if they do, those end users can get some of the benefits of PGP's model of operation by issuing a variety of certificates for themselves. They can also cross-sign certificates for other users, and that practice, if widely used, would lead to an X.509 web of trust.

The web of trust, whether expressed through PGP keys or certificates, seems well-suited to email that is sent between associates. It is less suitable for business relationships in which the customer has no previous interaction with the vendor. In that case, a trusted authority's signature on the business identity seems to be the only solution. Website identification is done through certificates issued by trusted authorities, and while the process is far from perfect, it probably protects against all but the most dedicated of fraudsters (Fig. 3.4).

Fig. 3.4 Conceptual PGP key packet and subkey packet

| Owner Public Key (large number) |
| User ID, a text string, usually an email address |
| Signature of Owner Public key over Subkey (large number) |
| Subkey Algorithm Type / Subkey Parameters (large number) |
| Signature of Subkey on Owner Public Key |
| Subkey's preferred Symmetric Cipher Algorithms |
| Signature of Subkey on Preferred Sym Algs |

What Makes Encrypted Email Secure?

Cryptography makes it impossible to forge signed email or to read encrypted email without knowing the keys. The keys should only be held by the owner of the email account. There are many factors that go into that assertion of "impossible", and much of the cryptologic research of the past 50 years stands behind it. There are four crucial pieces of cryptography that underly message security.

The primary technique for assuring email privacy is the symmetric cipher used to encrypt the data. Symmetric ciphers are designed with the goal of scrambling the data so well that there is no better method for decrypting the message than to try all possible keys. If the number of keys is astronomical, say 2^{128}, then this kind of brute force search is infeasible because there is not enough electric power on earth to run the computers that would do the search. Nonetheless, there are ciphers that have "super-astronomical" key spaces, such as 2^{256}, because sometime in the future there might be quantum computers that could search through all keys in ways that are impossible with today's computers.

The design and analysis of symmetric ciphers is part mathematics and part craft. There are three important properties: key size, speed of calculation, and resistance to attacks. Only the first two are easy to measure. Before 1990 there were not many ciphers that were really secure. They either had short keys, or an uncomfortably long time to compute, or turned out to have design flaws that opened them to attacks that could reveal the key or the message. Many cryptographers around the world took on the task of remedying the situation.

Since then, many good symmetric ciphers have entered into widespread use, and no attacks of significance have surfaced. The ciphers are well-suited to email usage because they encrypt and decrypt quickly on modern computers. The AES algorithm is a US government standard, suitable for business and personal use, and it has three key sizes: 128, 192, and 256 bits. The 3DES algorithm is an interesting holdover from the Pleistocene of cryptography. It is based on an algorithm from the 1970s that has a very short key (56 bits), but by running the algorithm 3 times with 3 different keys, it is as secure as if it had a 112-bit key, Some other ciphers with acceptable, time-tested security are CAMELLIA [23], and IDEA.

The symmetric cipher key is protected by public key algorithms and the analysis of the security of those is the subject of many learned papers. The problem comes down to two famous mathematical problems: factoring and discrete logarithms. The problems are deeply related, but not exactly the same. How hard are they to solve? In an absolute sense, we may never be able to answer that. On the other hand, some centuries of interest in the problems have yielded deep insights, and the insights have given rise to clever algorithms. How hard is it to compute someone's private RSA key from his public RSA key? It depends on the number of bits in the two primes that constitute the RSA modulus. As far as is known today, it might be possible to "break" a modulus of 1024 bits, but it has not been done. If we estimate the amount of work to carry out this Herculean task as 2^w, then the amount of work for a key of 8192 bits is 2^{2w}, a huge increase in effort.

Although symmetric ciphers with long keys sizes (256 bits or more) will still be secure in a world with quantum computers, the same is not true of the public key methods that are most commonly used today. The hard problems of factoring and discrete logs may not be so very difficult in the far technological future. The forecasting on this front is at best "through a glass darkly."

The way that you can be sure that a message has not been subjected to some kind of clever manipulation by an interloper is to check the modification detection code (MDC). An MDC is a fast way to summarize a block of data, and the one-way functions that are typically used for this are informally called "hash functions". Like symmetric ciphers, hash functions are as much art as science. They must be very fast and very difficult to manipulate. The probability of two different blocks of data having the same MDC must be astronomically miniscule. During the 1990s, the most commonly used hash function was MD5, but in 2004 its severe design flaws came to light. The SHA1 algorithm was the first good replacement for MD5, and it was widely adopted. Its reputation is dogged by unfulfilled claims of design weaknesses. Today, the SHA2 function is recommended as an MD5 replacement. A SHA3 algorithm is in the late stages of standardization by NIST [11], and it may become the recommended algorithm in the near future. No one expects to find devastating weaknesses in the design of either SHA2 or SHA3, but, like almost everything in practical cryptography, there is no guarantee of absolute security. The algorithms are designed to resist all known attack methods. They have fast software implementations on almost all computers. The algorithm evolution illustrates how balancing security against speed is as much art as science.

Another pillar of message security is the secrecy of the symmetric and private keys. It is more of an Achilles heel than a pillar. One problem with keys is the ubiquitous word "random" that occurs when people describe how the keys are generated by software. No matter how random the physical world seems, that randomness is difficult to capture in software. Many recent computers come with a special hardware instruction for producing random bits. There are other quasi-random things that a computer can access—the current time in microseconds, the time between key taps on a keyboard, the time between disk accesses, etc. All these things can be components of the "random bits" that underlie key generation. Some researchers have found problems with software that selects the two primes that are the basis for the RSA algorithms [13]. The primes must be unpredictable and secret for the key holder, but if the random number generator is weak, the primes could be easy to guess. In the worst case, the primes are reused for different users.

These components are the building blocks of secure email. The final step is putting it all together. Even when the pieces are the best possible, the details of secure message construction bedevil designers. For example, in its first incarnation, PGP did not use a modification detection code. After several years, cryptographers showed that the plaintext could sometimes be revealed by copying an encrypted message, changing it slightly, and sending it to the recipients. This would result in an error message to the sender that included some decrypted message text. Today, PGP uses a message detection code that prevents such occurrences.

A serious problem with certificates turned up when the widely used hash function MD5 was shown to have a serious flaw. It is important to avoid using MD5, but that is easier said than done because it is embedded so thoroughly in legacy software. To accommodate older systems, most systems today accept MD5 codes but do not generate them. The one critical exception is the use of MD5 as the basis for digital signatures. MD5 should never be trusted as part of a signature scheme.

After applying the best cryptographic algorithms to protect your email, you may expect that someone who finds the encrypted message on a server on the Internet will absolutely not be able to decrypt it, not now or anytime in the foreseeable future. Unless they discover your private key.

The private keys for RSA and DSA are the linchpin of the cryptographic secrecy; if the private key is disclosed, all past and current messages are vulnerable. How can someone keep their private key protected as a secret? Entrusting it to an ISP or an email service provider is not the the best way. But keeping it on your own computers is dangerous, as well. Keys are generally kept encrypted on the hard drive of a computer. When they are decrypted, they are kept in computer memory only for a short time. The key that is used to encrypt a key is generally called a "passphrase" to emphasize that it can be much longer than a single word. It is incumbent upon the user to choose a good passphrase and to avoid keeping the passphrase anywhere on a computer. Experts in digital forensics say that they can find passphrases in 99 % of all cases they investigate, so users must exercise a good deal of care to avoid making their passphrase readily available.

There is one aspect of communications security that email security does not address. Internet email has unencrypted data ("headers") that show the email address of the sender and the receiver and information about the pathway that the message took on its way to the delivery machine for the receiver. The communication patterns are valuable information, and governments collect this "metadata" for various kinds of surveillance operations. The Tor network [9] was built to frustrate traffic analysis. Its security is hard to quantify because it depends on the security of the individual nodes, and those may or may not be controlled by entities that collude to undermine the network.

Another problem facing a user is whether to trust attribution of the public key for encrypting email. Is it really Bob's key, or the key of someone pretending to be Bob? The nightmare scenario is that the key belongs to someone who intercepts and decrypts Bob's email, then re-encrypts it in Bob's real key and forwards it to him. The entire subject of how to establish trust on the Internet is one of the modern era's great unsolved problems. All ways of distributing keys depend on systems administered by humans with fallible judgment and error-prone procedures. Unless Alice and Bob sit down side-by-side and compare keys, there will always be the possibility of a corrupt key. This is, for most purposes, an acceptable risk, far superior to sending email that can be read by anyone.

Ciphers

Ciphers are what make encrypted email private. If you know the key, you can read it, if you don't, you can't. Of course, you also need to know what cipher was used. What cipher is used for encrypted email? There is no short answer—there are lots and lots of ciphers. This was not always true. When secure email started, in the 1970s, there were only a handful of symmetric ciphers and only two public key ciphers.

DES was the US government's published, approved cipher for protecting commercial data, including banking transactions and other sensitive information. The design decisions for DES were always shrouded in secrecy. Although the algorithm had been designed by mathematicians at IBM, it seemed to have some suspicious aspects, the most notable being its key length. By the 1990s, the 56-bit key was obviously not secure because it was feasible for an individual to build a machine that could search through all possible keys in a week or two. Today, an ordinary computer can do the same thing in a day or so. NIST embarked on a project to determine a more secure cipher via an open competition. The winner of that competition is today called AES, and it has key sizes far larger than 56 bits.

In order to allow the user community to strike a balance between security and speed of encryption, AES has three keysizes: 128, 192, and 256 bits. Larger keys are more secure, but smaller keys can encrypt and decrypt faster. By most measures, 128 bits is more than secure enough, but the larger sizes protect the most paranoid of users from future advances in computing technology.

Even beyond AES, today there are many ciphers that are fast and secure. The Camellia cipher was developed by Japanese researchers, and it has gained stamps of approval from a number of international standards bodies. Like AES, Camellia has three different key sizes. The Twofish cipher has stood up well to the test of time, and even the venerable 3DES algorithm continues to be a viable fall-back cipher for interoperability, despite its 112 bit key strength.

Is 128 bits enough to be secure? Yes. If the cipher has no structural weaknesses, the only available method of attack would be running through all possible keys, as was done for the 56-bit DES keys. Doing this for even one message would use a lot of electrical energy. If each computer operation used the minimum possible energy to move an electron from one orbit to another, the key search would use all the energy delivered to the surface of the earth from the sun for an entire year.

Even if we posit quantum computers capable of carrying out the search, some tiny amount of time is necessary for each operation. The current opinion of physicists is that examining a 256-bit keyspace with a quantum computer would be as difficult as doing the same for a 128-bit keyspace with the best possible traditional computer. If you are looking for "eternal encryption", a 256 bit key is good enough.

Public Key Signatures

We believe that public key signatures are secure because they are based on problems that mathematicians have worked on for centuries without finding any reason to think that they are easy solve by computer. The problems involve working with very, very large integers, something that computers are good at.

The security of public keys depends on the size of these integers. Public keys as large as 768 bits have been "broken" by concentrated computing efforts, but 1024 bits is arguably out of reach for a decade or two from now.

We have discussed the RSA signature/encryption algorithm previously because it is very easy to explain, but there are two others that are commonly used: DSA for signing [10, 28] and ElGamal for encryption [28].

It is convenient, before diving into DSA, to understand the Diffie-Hellman computation that lets Alice and Bob agree on a shared secret key. Alice and Bob first agree on a very large number prime number P to be their common modulus. They also agree on a generator, g (g is often the number 2). Alice selects a random number a from 1 to $P - 1$, and Bob similarly selects a number b. Alice calculates the very large number $g^a \bmod P$, and Bob similarly calculates $g^b \bmod P$. Alice and Bob might select different a and b numbers each time they communicate, or they might use the same numbers for some period of time. If Bob sends his large number $g^b \bmod P$ to Alice, then she can use that to calculate a shared key $k = (g^b)^a \bmod P$, and then she can encrypt the message m in key k using a symmetric cipher as described before. Her message to Bob is $\{g^a, encrypt\ (k, m)\}$. Bob can decrypt the message because he can use b to calculate $(g^a)^b \bmod P$, which is exactly the same number as $(g^b)^a \bmod P$. This fact is very important in public key cryptography and we will see it again in different settings.

Alice can publish an RSA key, and people can verify messages that she signs with it, but she can also publish a DSA key for the same purpose. The DSA algorithm is a little more difficult to explain, but it is very useful as an alternative to RSA. It also has a variation that lets people use shorter public keys.

In DSA, a public key consists of four numbers. Three of these are the parameters that can be reused. One is a prime number q of at least 128 bits in length, and another prime number p such that $(p - 1)$ is a large multiple of q. The number p should have at least 1532 bits. The third parameter is a number g that when raised to successive powers $mod\ p$, takes on q distinct values. Often the number $2^{(p-1)/q} \bmod p$ meets this requirement. The fourth number is based on a number a that is secret to the signer: $g^a \bmod P$. Alice can publish $\{q, p, g, g^a \bmod p\}$ as her public signing key; she holds the number a as her private key secret.

Alice uses the first three parameters of the her public key and her secret a to sign a short message m by first selecting a random number n between 0 and q. She uses n to calculate

$$r = (g^n \bmod p) \bmod q$$

compute the inverse, i, of $n \bmod q$ (this means to find a number i such that $i * n = 1$ *mod q*)

$$S = i * (m + a * r) \bmod q$$

[if either of r or S is zero, run the random number generator to select a new n].

The pair of numbers $\{r, S\}$ is the signature. Notice that r has both *mod p* and *mod q* in its computation. This is one of the oddest calculations that you are likely to see in cryptography!

Bob can verify Alice's signature on the message by using the four values in her public key. He begins by calculating the inverse of $S \bmod q = S^{-1}$. He then computes two values

$$c = m * S^{-1} \bmod q$$
$$d = r * S^{-1} \bmod q$$

Finally, he uses the remaining two values in the public key to compute

$$V = \left(\left(g^c * (g^a)^d \right) \bmod p \right) \bmod q$$

If the number r is equal to V, then the signature is verified.

If Alice ever reuses n, her private key a would be revealed, so she has to be very careful to use a good random number generator when she selects n.

The DSA scheme seems a lot more complicated than RSA, but it has a huge benefit. We won't go into the details, but any computation that is entirely based on powers of a generator in a *mod P* field can be done by analogy in a different kind of arithmetic. Elliptic curves are based on a fairly simple cubic equation. The equation has a two-dimensional representation as a curve. Surprisingly, two points on a curve can be "added" to produce a third curve point. The point's coordinates can be represented as rational numbers, and there is a formula that turns the coordinates of two points into the coordinates of a third point. If this "addition" is done *mod P*, then the points form a cyclic group, and there is a group generator, just as with normal integers. The upshot of this is that DSA can be computed over elliptic curve points in very much the same as it can on integers.

The important point about elliptic curves for cryptography is that the numbers don't have to be nearly as large as they do for the more common integer operations. For DSA, the larger prime number should be at least 1536 bits, but an elliptic curve of comparable security would have fewer than 200 bits in its corresponding calculations. This makes a big difference in the number of computer instructions for signing and for verification. Elliptic curve DSA (ECDSA) is much faster than plain DSA.

Public Key Encryption

In RSA, the number N is the result of multiplying two very large primes numbers together, but by contrast, in ElGamal, there is only one large prime number. That number, which should be at least 1536 bits long, will be denoted by the symbol P. There are numbers, called primitive roots of P, and Alice can choose one of them as her generator value, g. The generators have the property that their exponential powers, from 1 to $P - 1$, taken modulo $P - 1$, generate all the numbers from 1 to $P - 1$ in a different order. So Alice can select P, a generator g, and a random number that is less than $P - 1$. These three numbers define her ElGamal public key:

$$\text{Alice's public key} = \{P, g, (g^s \bmod P) = A\}$$

Bob can encrypt a short message m by selecting a random number b from 1 to $P - 1$ and using it to compute two values, g^b and A^b. He then takes his message m (which must be represented as a number from 1 to $P - 1$, and computes $m * A^b \bmod P$. His message to Alice consists of two pieces, $\{g^b, m * A^b\}$ (both numbers taken $\bmod P$) which Alice sees as two numbers $\{c_1, c_2\}$.

Alice can decrypt the message by using her secret value s to calculate $d = (c_1)^{-s} \bmod P$. Then, magically,

$$m = c_2 * d \bmod P.$$

Why does this work? It is because

$$A^b = g^{sb} \bmod P$$

and

$$(c_1)^{-s} = g^{-sb} \bmod P$$

When Alice multiplies d times c_2, she is dividing out the value that Bob created when he calculated A^b.

Notice that all the operations involve using a generator to a power. As we noted for DSA, this means that the computation for ElGamal can be done using elliptic curves. The cost saving in terms of computer instructions is significant, and the representation of the encrypted data is much smaller. Instead of using a prime P that is thousands of bits long, ElGamal based on elliptic curves only needs numbers that are fewer than 200 bits long. The security level is still excellent, exceeding the capabilities of any kind of computing environment available today or in the foreseeable future.

Identity-Based Encryption

One of the most interesting forms of public key encryption is based on a property of elliptic curves that is not shared by other forms of public key computation. Usually public keys are generated from a lengthy computation that must start at a large random number and search for a number with complicated properties. Suppose, though, that your name and email address easily could be turned into your public key? That would mean anyone could send encrypted email to you without looking up your public key. This is what identity-based encryption does.

The function that makes IBE work is one that preserves a homomorphism: one kind of computation using two elliptic curve points is exactly the same as another, different, computation using the same inputs. Suppose that there are two elliptic curve points, $P1$ and $P2$, and another pair $Q1$ and $Q2$, and a function e that operates on them while preserving two properties:

$$e(P1 + P2, Q1) = e(P1, Q1)e(P2, Q1)$$
$$e(P1, Q1 + Q2) = e(P1, Q1)e(P1, Q2)$$

Here e is a special kind of function called a pairing. It takes two points on an elliptic curve and maps them to a number in a finite field (note that it does *not* map the points to a third point). The two commonly used pairing functions are the Tate pairing and the Weil pairing, and both satisfy this property:

$$e(aP, \ bQ) = e(P, \ Q)^{ab}$$

This means that Bob can compute the right-hand side using one collection of information, and Alice can compute the right-hand side using different information. This is what gives rise to identity-based encryption.

The parameters of the system are an elliptic curve, a hash function, H, and a "trusted authority" with a well-known public key P, which is a point on the elliptic curve. The corresponding secret number s is known only the the trusted authority, but the point multiple of P, sP, is also public. Public keys are simplicity itself—the hash of whatever constitutes an *identity* is the public key of that entity. The corresponding private key, however, is known only to the trusted authority. By establishing a relationship with the trusted authority, a user can obtain his private key and thus claim his *identity*.

A public key is $H(ID) \rightarrow P'$, that is, the hash of the identity string is a point on the curve. The corresponding private key is sP'. Because s is a secret number known only to the trusted authority, the quantity sP' is a secret that the trusted authority sends to the holder of the identity ID using a secure transfer method. The identity holder should keep that key well-protected.

To send an IBE encrypted message m to "Bob <bob@example.com>", Alice maps the character string to a point on the published elliptic curve (let's call it B) by computing
  $H(\text{"Bob <bob@example.com>"}) = \text{IDBob} = B$
and then she chooses a random number r and then computes rB and rP.

She then computes $e(rB, sP) = k$ which is random point on the elliptic curve that will serve as the encryption key for the message m. Using a symmetric cipher, f, Alice computes $f(m, k)$ as the encryption of m. She sends rP and $f(m, k)$ to Bob.

Bob knows his secret key sB, and he can calculate k from rP by using a different equation:

$$e(sB, \ rP) = e(B, P)^{sr} = e(rB, sP) = k$$

Then Bob can use k to decrypt $f(m, k)$.

Because the IBE keys are based on elliptic curve points, they are shorter than RSA or DSA keys of equivalent security. Surprisingly, the pairing function e is not an elliptic curve computation, even though it takes elliptic curve points as inputs. Moreover, even a simple explanation of the function requires a heavy dose of advanced mathematics. If you are interested, look for definitions of the Weil pairing and the Tate pairing.

Voltage Security is a provider of IBE systems, and they have cloud-based systems for IBE email service. Despite its evident simplicity and clever side-stepping of all the problems of publishing and validating public keys, IBE has not caught on widely. Perhaps its lack of popularity stems from the reliance on a trusted authority. That trusted authority can compute anyone's secret key, and the integrity of that service underlies the security of the entire scheme.

What Does an Encrypted Message Look Like?

An encrypted message, if viewed in a text editor, appears to have no structure. It is a string of ascii characters with no meaning.

```
wYXvUWrHDy+41m8hvA3SCofDjqm7Zqh8Q95AQIFwBACNyhhm2krAhvcMZZbIHRNd (S/MIME)
```

or

```
iNlrDQ+lhAaJg2xhfpz6pG909DCz0xmxe3BBJKSFOmj16h6vCxEc4f/miMAJFUyZ (PGP)
```

These are the encoded formats that allow the messages to be sent over ordinary Internet email channels without confusing any of the underlying software. They can be decoded and read in their binary form, but that is not enlightening unless you are looking at the preamble material that describes the encryption algorithm, the public key method for encrypting the symmetric key, and the block of data that has the encrypted key. You can see these elements by using command line utilities—no key is necessary.

For OpenSSL and its ASN.1/CMS encoding, an example of how an encrypted message part is represented is shown here. The data begins with the certificate of the sender, then the certificate of the the CA, the RSA encryption of the symmetric key, the symmetric algorithm (aes-256-cbc) and its initial, random data (the initialization vector (IV) is a random number chosen afresh for each message):

```
   0:d=0  hl=4 l=2922 cons: SEQUENCE
   4:d=1  hl=2 l=   9 prim: OBJECT              :pkcs7-envelopedData
  43:d=8  hl=2 l=   9 cons: SEQUENCE
  45:d=9  hl=2 l=   3 prim: OBJECT              :countryName
  50:d=9  hl=2 l=   2 prim: PRINTABLESTRING     :US
  54:d=7  hl=2 l=  24 cons: SET
  56:d=8  hl=2 l=  22 cons: SEQUENCE
  58:d=9  hl=2 l=   3 prim: OBJECT              :organizationName
  63:d=9  hl=2 l=  15 prim: PRINTABLESTRING     :Paper, Inc.
  80:d=7  hl=2 l=  29 cons: SET
  82:d=8  hl=2 l=  27 cons: SEQUENCE
  84:d=9  hl=2 l=   3 prim: OBJECT              :organizationalUnitName
  89:d=9  hl=2 l=  20 prim: PRINTABLESTRING     :Dunder Miflin
 111:d=7  hl=2 l=  37 cons: SET
 113:d=8  hl=2 l=  35 cons: SEQUENCE
 115:d=9  hl=2 l=   3 prim: OBJECT              :organizationalUnitName
 120:d=9  hl=2 l=  28 prim: PRINTABLESTRING     :Scranton Office
 150:d=6  hl=2 l=   4 prim: INTEGER            :3C62B2A7
 156:d=5  hl=2 l=  13 cons: SEQUENCE
 158:d=6  hl=2 l=   9 prim: OBJECT              :rsaEncryption
 169:d=6  hl=2 l=   0 prim: NULL
 171:d=5  hl=4 l= 256 prim: OCTET STRING        [HEX
DUMP]:1A4E9B3FA694351C65DC3795BF102899D4CC7D12FD2E007A89204CF368E6FA5
1D31AEC235C9D53A7311E2011064D68DD5547C4F43C5E660463D9A17EC68C2CB87DCE
3A8E974F86C139F3AF73171DEF9E29660E40881B7CD9B47BF6922320F265AB762298A
EE7C3C01BFC7139CA3786DDC408D1D6F12B7B478FFF195DE4AB250AC83DFEC1ADE854
824ABF7FB23A953457A79AB9124C7479059B339A27D2BA9FCE3C29451E1CBFCD73D22
ED72A8D365AE3F43E04A3C87A6337B8D6C4027A442A531E16A68867723D7302E0EEE8
F87C32F1E70D2D6B0FD349FDC6578A1E5476F2116924F73A656EF3F265EAE0EC6DB72
13DA28301AFFB96DEEE9209F97F46D121F8
 431:d=4  hl=4 l= 457 cons: SEQUENCE
 435:d=5  hl=2 l=   1 prim: INTEGER            :00
 438:d=5  hl=3 l= 176 cons: SEQUENCE
 441:d=6  hl=3 l= 155 cons: SEQUENCE
 444:d=7  hl=2 l=  11 cons: SET
 446:d=8  hl=2 l=   9 cons: SEQUENCE
 448:d=9  hl=2 l=   3 prim: OBJECT              :countryName
 453:d=9  hl=2 l=   2 prim: PRINTABLESTRING     :GB
 457:d=7  hl=2 l=  27 cons: SET
 459:d=8  hl=2 l=  25 cons: SEQUENCE
 461:d=9  hl=2 l=   3 prim: OBJECT              :stateOrProvinceName
 466:d=9  hl=2 l=  18 prim: PRINTABLESTRING     :Surrey
 486:d=7  hl=2 l=  16 cons: SET
 488:d=8  hl=2 l=  14 cons: SEQUENCE
 490:d=9  hl=2 l=   3 prim: OBJECT              :localityName
 495:d=9  hl=2 l=   7 prim: PRINTABLESTRING     :Port Wenn
 504:d=7  hl=2 l=  26 cons: SET
 506:d=8  hl=2 l=  24 cons: SEQUENCE
 508:d=9  hl=2 l=   3 prim: OBJECT              :organizationName
 513:d=9  hl=2 l=  17 prim: PRINTABLESTRING     :Root CA,Inc.
 532:d=7  hl=2 l=  65 cons: SET
 534:d=8  hl=2 l=  63 cons: SEQUENCE
 536:d=9  hl=2 l=   3 prim: OBJECT              :commonName
 541:d=9  hl=2 l=  56 prim: PRINTABLESTRING     :Root CA SHA-256 Client
                              Authentication and Secure Email CA
 599:d=6  hl=2 l=  16 prim: INTEGER          5ADAC54C3788801A24799C620466CAB7
```

```
617:d=5  hl=2 l=  13 cons: SEQUENCE
619:d=6  hl=2 l=   9 prim: OBJECT            :rsaEncryption
630:d=6  hl=2 l=   0 prim: NULL
632:d=5  hl=4 l= 256 prim: OCTET STRING - the encrypted AES key [HEX DUMP]:
27F919EF14DE88A20D72E572FD30BBADF7D2EF069F8EE9BF090BEFE127955ABDE3385CD91F7FD
C3D38603541E221AAC58BAF67A88DDB7CED517D87F13F6D52F3692028DF52A9B5D1E548594CCE
EE57CC048832FC0A8C86FA43C7B14D2C6CF4117B75521A361F1EDFF53CE05290C5D175A0943FB
4AEA04C0010B9B38C8B48C488294F073141989B66C1D1BBD6B47B57FA025168132FE823AB838FC
1FC286ECD1EA6297B0519C0B5A305FCAAFD22156E708355D46C9F5D3EF843A058066696529CD9
ECDEF11A312622B47B55AA72706644A8FC95C351C36C8740B67FA284FD0EAAF8A2C7A0CF4EAB0
F1A0EC9A439EFCAB70C1DB3AB517F54C2D3B59A8D8B1008C2
 892:d=3  hl=4 l=2030 cons: SEQUENCE
 896:d=4  hl=2 l=   9 prim: OBJECT            :pkcs7-data
 907:d=4  hl=2 l=  29 cons: SEQUENCE
 909:d=5  hl=2 l=   9 prim: OBJECT            :aes-256-cbc
 920:d=5  hl=2 l=  16 prim: OCTET STRING --- the Initialization Vector
                            [HEXDUMP]:5151EF74545848F02244C444139B74AD
 938:d=4  hl=4 l=1984 prim: cont [ 0 ]
(the next 1984 bytes would be the encrypted message text)
```

The pgpdump utility software reveals the internal structure of the PGP packets, though not in the detail of the OpenSSL example. The following data shows the representation of the information for an message encrypted with AES with a 256 bit key, that key encrypted with the 2044 bit RSA subkey of a public key packet for a 1024 bit ElGamal signing key.

```
Old: public key Encrypted Session Key Packet(tag 1)(268 bytes)
     New version(3)
     Key ID - 0x5CB5D88711C1D389
     Pub alg - RSA Encrypt or Sign(pub 1)
     RSA m^e mod n(2044 bits) - ...
          -> m = sym alg(1 byte) + checksum(2 bytes) + PKCS-1 block type 02
Old: public key Encrypted Session Key Packet(tag 1)(270 bytes)
     New version(3)
     Key ID - 0xC61923251C50FA4E
     Pub alg - ElGamal Encrypt-Only(pub 16)
     ElGamal g^k mod p(1024 bits) - ...
     ElGamal m * y^k mod p(1024 bits) - ...
          -> m = sym alg(1 byte) + checksum(2 bytes) + PKCS-1 block type 02
New: Symmetrically Encrypted and MDC Packet(tag 18)(209 bytes)
     Ver 1
     Encrypted data [sym alg is specified in pub-key encrypted session key]
          (plain text + MDC SHA1(20 bytes))
     AES encrypted data
       :compressed packet: algo=2
       :literal data packet:
       mode b (62), created 1423437599, name="",
       raw data: 191 bytes
```

The packet types are defined in RFC 4880. For example, packet tag 18 is "Sym. Encrypted Integrity Protected Data Packet". As noted in the detail, the algorithm is encoded in the session key (in the first byte). It is evident that PGP encodes its packets in a scheme different from CMS, but the details are all described in the RFC.

S/MIME Headers

As with the original PEM design, S/MIME has two kinds of signing: (1) message is readable by non-SMIME software, (2) message cannot be read by non-S/MIME clients. You may have received messages of the former type without even realizing it. If you received a "signed data" message, you would be aware of it because those cannot be read unless you have S/MIME software that will decode the data and separate the signature from the message. In the first type of message, the signature is "detached" in that it is a message part separate from the readable text.

You may well have certificates from these "detached signature" messages in your key manager, even if you yourself have never sent a single secure email.

Example Header (before message parts):

```
Content-Type: multipart/signed;

boundary="Apple-Mail=_82AEDE9E-D087-4F75-B6DE-985766DCF295";

        protocol="application/pkcs7-signature"; micalg=sha1
```

An example of an interior part, delimited by boundary above:

```
Content-Type: application/pkcs7-signature; name="smime.p7s"
```

The OpenSSL software utilities are invaluable tools for examining message structures and debugging problems. The software can create and parse S/MIME messages, the certificates, the CMS data structures, etc.

One of the many uses is to extract the certificates from an encrypted message. If the certificate chain is not completely contained in the message, for example, this can help in understanding why it is marked as "not trusted" by email software.

To manually look at a base64 decoded p7s attachment from a message in the file jane-binary:

```
openssl pkcs7 -in jane-binary -inform DER -out jane-cert.txt -print_certs
```

To annually look at the certificate block printed by the previous command:

```
openssl x509 -in jane-cert.txt -noout -text
```

S/MIME signed messages can include additional, useful security information about the signer's security preferences, and recipients of these messages can refer to previously signed messages to find the preferred algorithms for that correspondent. That information is encoded in the SMIMECapabilities attribute. Most S/MIME users do not have direct control over what the email client sends in the attribute, nor do they see what their correspondents have put into their capabilities attribute. Senders have implicit control through the user profile settings and the base set of required algorithms (e.g., RSA signatures are generally required, as is the 3DES symmetric encryption algorithm). Drawing on experience from the history of encryption deployments on the Internet, the S/MIME designers allowed for extensions to the capabilities attribute.

Chapter 4
Using Secure Email

Anyone who has a public key can start using secure email. Just what kind of key you can use depends on your email software and the email software of your recipients. Using secure email today is a combination of ease and frustration. The ease comes from having the "sign" and "encrypt" options easily available from the application menus. It is also automatic to have incoming messages verified and decrypted. Almost all email clients today have this capability, and most of them support both S/MIME and PGP. The major exception to this is, unfortunately, Microsoft's Outlook. The standard version of Outlook supports only S/MIME and certificates.

The frustration in secure email comes largely from the key management. Keys are not built into email clients. Getting a key for your own use is a bit mysterious. Sending your public key to another person is easy to do but "non-obvious". Getting someone else's key is a problem with a variety of solutions. Convincing your own key management software that you want to incorporate someone else's public encryption key into your tools for sending email is maddening. Moving all the information about keys from one device to another is not easy, because the email system thinks that function is the responsibility of the key management application. Removing keys that are expired or out of date is troublesome. Remembering the passphrase for unlocking your key is difficult. And the Internet is littered with keys for which no one remembers the password or has the corresponding private key. The information gets lost when moving to a new machine, recovering from a hard drive crash, or just forgetting about it.

You can distribute your certificate or PGP key by posting it on a website, including it as an email attachment, or sharing it at a "key signing party", or any other means of sharing data. When someone gives you a key, you will have to import it into your key management system. Usually you can do this by opening the key manager application and using the "import" function to import a key for another person.

You should start by sending a signed email, because you only need your signing key for this, you do not need to have your recipient's key. If you are using S/MIME, your signature will contain your certificate information in an "smime.p7s" attachment. If you have email with signatures in your inbox, try viewing those certificates in a key manager. You can also view certificates in your browser's certificate store—although they are not usable for email, you may be surprised at how many certificates you have collected and the variety of certificate authorities.

© The Author(s) 2015
H. Orman, *Encrypted Email*,
SpringerBriefs in Computer Science,
DOI 10.1007/978-3-319-21344-6_4

When you start using secure email features, you will need to go through the following steps to get your identity established and to let your correspondents know that you are a secure email user. If you are using both S/MIME and PGP, you will need to go through the steps for each of them.

- Import your key
- Send a signed email
- Send your public key
- Receive and verify a signed email
- Import a correspondent's key
- Send encrypted email
- Receive encrypted email
- Move your keys to a new device

The following sections cover the operations needed to start using secure email on several different email applications. The information may not be complete or definitive, but in conjunction with the information about how secure email works and what it is intended to do, users should have enough information to work through the details of any system. There are a variety of materials on the Internet that are helpful, and users should look for technical reports from the application providers for additional help with the exact version of the software being used. Not all information has equal value, and in some cases the sheer volume of advice can lead to frustration. Most of the information that one will encounter online make sense if the reader is firmly grounded in the basics of secure email's purposes and mechanisms.

Outlook

Over the last several years the Outlook menus that lead to the security options have changed multiple times. Users should look for the "Trust Center" and the "Email Security" options. The place to start is the "Tools" menu. On older systems, try "File" and "Options".

In the Trust Center or Advanced Options, you can import your personal keys from "backup" files (the .p12 files for exported private keys and certificate chains). You can associate the keys with your email account, and you can use them for signing email and for decrypting email sent to you.

Accounts can be configured to sign and/or encrypt messages by default. On the other hand, the user can select these functions for a new message by using the "Options" tab while composing the message. The S/MIME sign and S/MIME encrypt options are always there, under "security options for this message". The security enhancements are applied when the user hits "send".

Your "Sent" folder will hold the encrypted message, but unless you "cc"d yourself, you will not be able to read the message. And if you do "cc" yourself, you might run into the problem of getting your own email software to trust your own keys!

When displaying a received S/MIME message, Outlook will display an icon indicating that the message is signed and/or encrypted. When you click on the icon, the verification status will be displayed for a signed message, and the plaintext of the message will be displayed if it was an encrypted message.

Outlook does not handle PGP messages. There is, however, a PGP extension for Outlook from the GPG developers. If you install this software, it integrates nicely with Outlook, albeit not quite in parallel with S/MIME. For example, when sending a message, the PGP sign and encrypt functions are under the "Format" tab. When sending a message, you will have the chance to select the PGP key that you want to use for signing or encrypting.

Thunderbird

Thunderbird is a widely available email client that handles both PGP and S/MIME messages.

In Thunderbird on MacOS, the certificate management for S/MIME is handled through the standard application "Keychain Access". This handles more than just email keys, but you will find that keys from your correspondents will show up in that application without any intervention on your part. You can import and export your own certificates and use them for signing and decrypting email.

Support for GPG can be added to Thunderbird easily. The GPG website has distributions and instructions.

When sending a message, the composing window will have a small triangle on the upper righthand corner. You can select signing and/or encryption enhancements to the message using that tab.

Evolution

The Evolution email client has support for both PGP and S/MIME. You can associate a PGP key or S/MIME "backup" certificate with your account.

When you are composing a message you can select from "S/MIME signed", "S/MIME encrypted", "PGP signed", and "PGP encrypted". The signed and encrypted options can be combined for either S/MIME or PGP.

The signature is verified if you click on the message; if it can be decrypted it will be processed and displayed as plaintext. Signatures can be validated, but the certificate might not be backed by a full certificate chain, or it might not have a trusted root authority. Those conditions will result in a validation failure or warning message. The manual utilities for examining messages and certificates can be used to get additional information to help settle these puzzling cases.

Apple Mobile Devices (iOS)

The "Mail" app that is pre-installed on Apple's iOS devices has the capability to handle S/MIME. The only problem is finding the controls to turn it on.

Under "Settings", and "Mail", each "Account" has a tab. If an account is selected, there is a menu for detailed configuration of its sending and receiving configuration, and at the bottom of that menu there is an "Advanced" tab. Continuing to the "Advanced" menu, the user will see, at the very bottom, the "S/MIME" options for sign and encrypt. Selecting "yes" for either one brings up one more menu for selecting the certificate to use for the account. If you previously have imported a certificate and key by sending yourself a "p12" file, you will see that item listed as an option.

You cannot select sign or encrypt for individual messages because it is a property of the entire account and applies to all message that you send.

Signed or encrypted messages that are delivered to the account are automatically processed. Helpful icons show if the incoming signature is verified.

Personal certificates and private keys for the user can be imported by emailing a password protected file in "p12" format to oneself. Opening the attachment invokes the certificate management software for the device, and the password will open the file and ask if you want to trust the certificate and key.

The main problem with the iOS software is that if something fails, there is little information to use in trying to understand and fix the problem.

There are PGP email apps for iOS. They do not share data with the pre-installed email application, so there may be some inconvenience in trying to manage both systems. Even if you only send email from using S/MIME, you may want to install PGP capability for verifying signed messages from PGP-only users.

Android

The Android operating system does not have secure email options within its usually pre-installed "Email" app. The operating system understands S/MIME formats, and a certificate bundle in "p12" format can be imported onto the device using a web browser. Native security enhancements for email may be available in the near future. In the meantime, third-party apps for PGP and S/MIME are readily available.

Regardless of the mobile device type, users should be careful about keeping their certificates and keys protected with a good, non-guessable passphrase.

Not Everything Is Smooth

For ordinary email, there are relatively few serious problems. An email message might bounce, or sometimes the system might not be able to read some kind of multimedia attachment, and everyone gets too much spam, but encrypted email can inflict a whole new world of pain. If it works, it is easy, but there are many problems that cannot be solved without a fairly deep knowledge of the architecture and implementation of the methods.

For S/MIME, the p7s signature might not have a complete certificate chain. This probably happens because the sender's email provider or administrator did not anticipate having the email security extend outside the organization's boundaries. The email can be verified with respect to the sender's certificate, but the full certificate chain is inaccessible. To verify the message without the full chain, you can use OpenSSL "cert" utilities.

For PGP, the sender's key is not usually part of the signature. You need to decode the signature and find the key id, then use your key manager to search the PGP website(s) to find the key id. You can decide if the key is trustworthy based on either the signatures on the key, or by the usage context—if it is a mailing list, you might ask other people on the list if they trust the key.

Sometimes you will receive a message encrypted in a key that your email application does not recognize. This usually happens when you have forgotten to import the key to a new machine, but it also can happen if someone finds an old key for you on a PGP server, or if the correspondent has not been in touch with you for some years. You can use command line tools to find the information that identifies the key used for encryption, and if it is an outdated key, you should send your current key information to the correspondent. If it is a current key, make sure that you have imported it to your current email client.

Certificates sometimes seem unwieldy and cumbersome. Even if you have corresponded previously with someone and used their certificate at one time, later uses might fail. Here is a list of hints from RFC 5750 "Secure/Multipurpose Internet Mail Extensions (S/MIME) Version 3 Certificate Handling":

Some of the many places where signature and certificate checking might fail include:

- no Internet mail addresses in a certificate match the sender of a message (if the certificate contains at least one mail address)
- no certificate chain leads to a trusted CA
- no ability to check the CRL for a certificate
- an invalid CRL was received
- the CRL being checked is expired
- the certificate is expired
- the certificate has been revoked

Even if all these are satisfied, not everyone will be enamored of your certificate. Some sites will not accept a certificate if any of the CA keys in the chain have expired. Some systems will be configured to deny users the ability to add new root authorities or self-signed certificates. Your mileage may vary.

Even if the software is satisfied with all the keys and the trust relationships, and your email has been sent, there can still be a major security problem: was the email actually encrypted? This is difficult to answer, because if it was not encrypted, there is no error message that results. Only manual inspection of the message that was actually sent can give a satisfactory answer. The command line tools for OpenSSL and GPG are very helpful in this regard because they can provide a parsed version of messages in the "Sent" folder.

Because S/MIME and PGP can protect individual message parts, it can be particularly difficult to determine if a binary attachment of a photograph, for example, is actually encrypted. This problem turned up in some versions of secure email for Apple's iOS email client. The software encrypted the text part of messages, but not the attachments [20]. This was discovered by someone who looked at a message dissection in detail. The problem was fixed in subsequent releases of the operating system, but it all goes to show that you cannot be too careful.

General advice:

- Realize that your key manager and your email client might not be in synch. You may need to restart one or the other after importing new keys for yourself or other correspondents.
- You should configure your email client to use a particular certificate and/or PGP for each account.
- The key management system will not trust a certificate authority to authenticate email users unless you explicitly tell it to do so. PGP similarly requires you to sign a key before you can use it to encrypt a message to the owner.
- In case of failure, you can use command line tools of openSSL or PGP to debug, repair, and retry the security features.
- Error messages might be obscure, even "cryptic". Internet search tools are your friends.

A Key of One's Own

To get started with email security you must have a public key. Not only does the public key make it possible for you to sign email and receive encrypted email, it is also a signal to the email system to enable the options for all public key operations, including verifying the signatures on email that you receive.

You probably have, at some time, received signed email. You might not have noticed the mysterious attachment name—a little note about "smime.p7s" or "signature.asc". If you don't have a public key yourself, your email reader probably hasn't taken the trouble to verify the message against the signature. Once you have a public key of your own, this can change, and verified messages will get special markings in your inbox—a star or other icon, and informative text near the message indicating that "this message is verified".

If your employer uses an enterprise security product, you might have a key automatically associated with your email account. If not, or if you are looking for a key for use with a personal email account, there are several paths to follow. Keep in mind that you need two key pairs to play in the secure email game: a public/private key pair for signing and a public/private key pair for encrypting. Almost any key generation method described here automatically generates both pairs and marks one as the signing key pair and the other as the encryption key pair.

The following sections frequently mention using a key management application to import or export keys or certificates and to manage them by assigning trust to them, etc. The controls for these functions are sometimes contained entirely within an email application, but sometimes they are shared with a separate application that manages keys for all applications on the computer. For the Apple MacOS system, the "Keychain" application handles certificates and the associated keys; when the Gnu Privacy Guard software is installed there is a second application, "GPG Keychain Access". On Linux systems, the "Seahorse" key manager is one of a number of applications for managing PGP keys; support for certificates comes through email clients and/or OpenSSL utilities. Microsoft Windows systems manage email keys adequately through Outlook and supported web browsers. You may need to experiment with your preferred applications to see how to perform the required functions most easily.

Certificate and Key Generation Method 1: Apply to a Certificate Authority

Various commercial entities offer certificates as a product, especially for website authentication, but email certificates are also available. The advantage of the service is that you get an X.509v3 certificate signed by an entity that is part of a clique of highly trusted issuers. Their signature on a certificate is likely to make the certificate "trusted" by any software that deals with them.

In an ideal world, the user of such services would generate a key pair on his own computer and present the public key to the certificate issuing service for signing. There is a PKCS format for representing a public key and identifying information in a file for presentation to a certificate authority; this is a "certificate signing request" (csr). However, in some cases the issuer generates the key pair and delivers it to the user over a trusted connection. Of course, the issuer might have kept a copy of the private key, thus negating the user's desire to have complete control over his own privacy. The convenience might overweigh the insecurity for some users.

One way to get a public key is to apply to a top-level certificate authority (TLCA) for a free key pair with an X.509v3 certificate. At the current time,

Comodo offers this service. Their website has an application form where you can enter your name and email address, and they will mail you a link to get access to the certificate with the key pair. When you get the email, make sure that the link is for Comodo (look at the browser's "lock" icon and make sure that it is an "https" secure connection). When you click on the link, the certificate is delivered to you through your browser's certificate management system. This is a confusing procedure because you probably never realized that your browser had such a thing. When you visit websites that identify themselves through certificates, your browser silently checks the validity of those certificates and puts them into an internal data store. Your personal Comodo certificate is delivered to you the same way. You will need to use your passphrase from the registration step as part of retrieving the certificate package.

In order to use the certificate for email, you will need to find it through your browser controls and "export" it.

In Firefox, the certificate store is hidden in "Preferences", and then "Advanced". Most everything related to cryptography is under the "Advanced" section in any browser or email application. Beyond "Advanced" you will proceed to "Security" and then "Certificates" and then "Your certificates".

The term "certificate" is a misnomer in this context, because what you have is a PKCS#12 encrypted "package" consisting of two certificates for you (containing public keys) signed by Comodo and the corresponding private keys. One certificate has a signing key, the other has an encryption key. The package is encrypted using a passphrase that you supply during the registration process with Comodo. In addition to this, you will get Comodo's self-signed top-level CA certificate.

To get the certificates out of the encrypted package and into the form that you can share with others, you need to "export" the certificates into a file. It will usually be stored in "PEM" format (one of the remaining artifacts of "Privacy Enhanced Mail").

Your certificate has been signed by the top-level certificate authority (in this case, Comodo). Their signing key has to be available to anyone who wants to validate your public key, so their self-signed certificate is part of the PKCS#12 encrypted package. You might wonder how someone else will know that Comodo is a top-level CA. The answer is that it either built into their certificate management software, or they will have to add Comodo if they wish to trust your certificate.

Along with the certificates, your browser has the all-important private keys, and before using them in an email client, you will need to copy them into an encrypted file on your computer. The file extension for public/private key usually has the file extension ".p12". To encrypt the file, you will be prompted to provide a passphrase. Make a note of the passphrase, because if you forget it, you will lose the ability to decrypt email sent to you. The operation that writes the p12 files has a confusing name: backup. The notion is that you are creating a backup copy of your key information—both the private and public.

Some browsers have their certificate and key management integrated with other applications, particularly with an email reader. This may mean that the process of receiving the certificate through a weblink automatically makes it available to an email reader. However, if you want to use that key on a different device, you probably will need to "backup" the key and mail it to yourself as an attachment (do not forget the passphrase!).

After you have exported your certificates and keys, you will be able to use them in your email client. If the signing key does not show up as an option when you try to use S/MIME signing for an email message, then go to the certificate management options for the email client and use the "import" function to incorporate the p12 file into your email client and/or key manager. You will *again* need the passphrase.

Certificate and Key Generation, Method 2: OpenSSL and X.509v3 Certificates

A more secure method for generating keys and certificates is to "do-it-yourself" with the open source software OpenSSL. There are key management GUIs that simplify this process, but in this section we will cover the command line interface that provides detailed control over the process. Even if you do use a GUI app to generate and manage your keys, OpenSSL provides ways to examine and control the details of your keys.

Because OpenSSL is based on the PKI system of hierarchical certificates, the first step in the do-it-yourself method is to create a certificate authority of your own. In the second step, you will issue a certificate to yourself, the third step describes using the key in your email program, and the fourth step will be to tell your colleagues how they can trust you as a CA.

Step 1: Create a Certificate Authority

Openssl has hundreds of possible parameters, and they can be used to carry out almost any key management or encryption task, if you know how to use them. Because it is so complicated, everyone looks for online examples to find the magic formulas. In this section we will go through the process as succinctly as possible. There are are applications that bundle the commands into a simpler set of inter-actions, but there is value in understanding the underlying structures in the event that you need to examine the results or make changes. The most common change, of course, will be to renew the certificates after the expiration period.

Before creating any certificates, it is useful to make a configuration file for your CA. The configuration file describes the identifying information for your CA and the information that you will require for certificates that you create. It also describes where you will put some crucial information files and what they will be named. Figure 4.1 shows a simple configuration file for a hypothetical CA:

```
dir                         = .
[ ca ]
default_ca                  = CA_default

[ CA_default ]
serial                      = $dir/serial
database                    = $dir/certindex.txt
new_certs_dir               = $dir/certs
certificate                 = $dir/ps-cacert.pem
private_key                 = $dir/private/ps-cakey.pem
default_days                = 730
default_md                  = sha1
preserve                    = no
email_in_dn                 = yes
nameopt                     = default_ca
certopt                     = default_ca
policy                      = policy_match

[ policy_match ]
countryName                 = match
stateOrProvinceName         = match
organizationName            = match
organizationalUnitNam       = optional
commonName                  = supplied
emailAddress                = optional

[ req ]
default_bits                = 2048         # Size of keys
default_keyfile             = key.pem      # name of
generated keys
default_md                  = sha1         # message
digest algorithm
string_mask                 = nombstr      # permitted
characters
distinguished_name          = req_distinguished_name
req_extensions              = v3_req

[ req_distinguished_name ]
# Variable name                     Prompt string
#----------------------      ---------------------------
0.organizationName           = Organization Name (company)
organizationalUnitName       = Organizational Unit Name
                               (department, division)
emailAddress                 = Email Address
```

Fig. 4.1

```
emailAddress_max              = 40
localityName                  = Locality Name (city, district)
stateOrProvinceName           = State or Province Name (full name)
countryName                   = Country Name (2 letter code)
countryName_min               = 2
countryName_max               = 2
commonName                    = Common Name (hostname,IP,
                                or your name)
commonName_max                = 64

# Default values for the above, for consistency and lesstyping.
# Variable name                    Value
#----------------------    ------------------------------
0.organizationName_default       = Dunder Mifflin
localityName_default             = Scranton
stateOrProvinceName_default      = PA
countryName_default              = US

[ v3_ca ]
basicConstraints              = CA:TRUE
subjectKeyIdentifier          = hash
authorityKeyIdentifier        = keyid:always,issuer:always


[ v3_req ]
basicConstraints              = CA:FALSE
subjectKeyIdentifier          = hash
```

Fig. 4.1 (continued)

This command establishes your CA certificate:

```
openssl req -new -x509 -extensions v3_ca -keyout private/ps-cakey.pem -out \
   ps-cacert.pem -config ./ps.conf
```

Step 2: Issue a certificate

Start by creating a new key that will be signed by the certificate authority. In the following, an elliptic curve signing key using a built-in 256-bit prime is generated:

```
openssl ecparam -genkey -name prime256v1 -out eckey2.pem
```

Next create the data structure with a request to have the key signed. This step prepares the key material to be presented to a Certificate Authority for signing. You will supply your organization name, real name, and email address:

```
openssl req -new -key eckey2.pem -out ec2-csr.pem
```

The output file, ec2-csr.pem, is the PEM encoded request. That can be signed by your local CA, or another CA, using this command:

```
openssl ca -out ec2-cert.pem -config ./ps.conf -infiles ec2-csr.pem
```

Assuming that you remembered and used all your passphrases correctly you now have a signed certificate in the file ec2-cert.pem.

Step 3: Incorporate the key into your email client

In order to use your new key in an email client you need to create a file that has your signed certificate and the private key. Both things already exist through the operations carried out in the previous steps, but they have to be combined into one file and password protected. The PKCS standard for this kind of file is known as PKCS#12 and the file extension is "p12" or "pfx". The OpenSSL command for creating these files is part of the pkcs subsystem, and the important operation is "export":

```
openssl pkcs12 -export -in ec2-cert.pem -inkey eckey2.pem -out eckey2.p12
```

Somewhere, under some tab, your email client will have a menu for managing keys. In Evolution it is under "Edit/Preferences/Certificates". Your objective is to "import" the key that you just "exported". There are three classes of certificates that could be imported: a certificate for you to use with your own identity when sending email, a certificate for a correspondent, or a certificate for a "root authority". For the first type of certificate, you will need a file with extension "p12", and that is what was created with the "openssl pkcs12" command.

Select the "import" operation for "my certificates", give it the pathname of your eckey2.p12 file, and click, "import".

Step 4: Use your new certificates and keys for email

You can start signing email with your new key immediately. Select "SMIME sign", and send an email to one of your correspondents. The SMIME signature will be an attachment of type "p7s", and it will contain your signature, your certificates for that key and your encryption key, and a certificate for the "root CA" you created in step 1. Your correspondents will probably get a warning message about the root CA not being in their list of trusted CAs.

Your correspondents will have to find your CA certificate in their list of "certificates for others", and they should import that certificate to their CA list. You will have to do the same for your correspondents who create their own CAs.

After importing your certificates, your correspondents can use the key management system to indicate that they trust your keys for signing and encrypting. Then, they can send encrypted messages to you.

Certificate and Key Generation, Method 3: Generate a PGP Key

PGP software is widely available, and PGP keys are easy to generate. The free software version of PGP is the GNU Privacy Guard (GPG), and we will use it to illustrate key generation.

There are GUI-based key managers that simplify key generation. For example, there is "GPG Keychain Access" for Apple MacOS devices. To use it, you simply enter your name and email address. If you want more control over the process, you can select "Advanced" and choose the key types and lengths and expiration period. The key will be generated and added to your list of available keys ("keychain").

You can also generate a key from a command line interface. This has the advantage of letting you see advisory messages during key generation. For example, the software must "gather entropy" before generating a key, and the longer the key, the more entropy is needed, and thus more time is required. It is not uncommon to see a message during key generation about needing to wait for more activity on the computer before the required entropy is available. Several minutes might go by. If you are using the GUI, you might think the process was "stuck" and try to start over. Don't.

We'll go through key generation from the command line so that we can discuss the effect of choosing different options.

```
gpg --gen-key

Please select what kind of key you want:
   (1) RSA and RSA (default)
   (2) DSA and Elgamal
   (3) DSA (sign only)
   (4) RSA (sign only)
```

What this means is that for options 1 and 2, you will get two keys, one for signing and one for encryption. You can choose to have both of those be RSA keys, or you can have a DSA signing key and an ElGamal encryption key. Options 3 and 4 are for signing keys only. Either option 1 or 2 is what you will need for email. There is no option here for elliptic curve keys; they are relatively new to GPG, and you can find them in the most recent releases of GPG (versions 2.1 and higher).

Select the key type. For illustration purposes, assume that option 2 is selected.

```
DSA keys may be between 1024 and 4096 bits long.
What keysize do you want? (2048)
```

Hit return to accept the default value of 2048 bits. Although you can choose longer keys of either 3072 or 4096 bits, these can bog down your computer if you process a lot of complex email. The extra security of longer keys is not necessary at the current time.

```
Please specify how long the key should be valid.
         0 = key does not expire
      <n>  = key expires in n days
      <n>w = key expires in n weeks
      <n>m = key expires in n months
      <n>y = key expires in n years
```

Key is valid for? (0) 2y

Two years is a reasonable expiration time; shorter time spans will only cause trouble, and long ones run the risk of having the key forgotten and or compromised some years down the line. If you use a calendar reminder system, set a reminder for two years in the future to "renew PGP email certicate".

```
You need a user ID to identify your key; the software constructs the user ID
from the Real Name, Comment and Email Address in this form:
    "Heinrich Heine (Der Dichter) <heinrichh@duesseldorf.de>"
```

Unless you are Heinrich Heiner, you'll want to first enter your name as you want others to see it.

```
Real name: Alice T. Smith
```
Your email address is next

```
Email address: atsmith@example.com
```

Then a comment if necessary

```
Comment: For testing only

You selected this USER-ID:
    "Alice T. Smith <atsmith@example.com>"

Change (N)ame, (C)omment, (E)mail or (O)kay/(Q)uit?
```

If everything is OK, enter "O".

```
You need a Passphrase to protect your secret key.
Enter passphrase:
```

This is a big nuisance. Despite all the convenience of public key methods, the private key is the Achilles heel of the system, and you have to protect it from accidental disclosure. The private key will be encrypted with a symmetric cipher while it is stored on your hard drive. The passphrase will be used to generate an encryption key. Choose a good passphrase and make sure you can remember it. Write it down somewhere, otherwise you will surely forget it and you will never be able to read encrypted email that you receive. Enter the passphrase, then enter it again when prompted. You will then see some complicated text describing information in your key database:

```
gpg: key B5565A34 marked as ultimately trusted
public and secret key created and signed.

gpg: checking the trustdb
gpg: 3 marginal(s) needed, 1 complete(s) needed, PGP trust model
gpg: depth: 0  valid:   5  signed:   3  trust: 0-, 0q, 0n, 0m, 0f, 5u
gpg: depth: 1  valid:   3  signed:   0  trust: 0-, 0q, 0n, 0m, 3f, 0u
gpg: next trustdb check due at 2015-10-14
pub   2048D/B5565A34 2015-03-11 [expires: 2017-03-10]
      Key fingerprint = 357A 6B81 E259 ED13 5DAA  200D 1781 1CDB B556 5A34
uid                  Alice T. Smith <atsmith@example.com>
sub   2048g/530BAE58 2015-03-11 [expires: 2017-03-10]
```

The first two lines let you know that you created a key pair, and the key identifier for the public key is "B5565A3". That identifier is derived from the public key, and it is unlikely but possible that two different keys can have the same identifier. Because you generated the key yourself, it is trusted at the maximum level of "ultimate".

The line that begins "pub" indicates that you have a public key of length 2048 bits with the key idenfier noted earlier, the day is was created, and the day it expires. The "Key fingerprint" is a unique identifier for the key, and the last 8 characters are the short identifier. This is the identifier for the public key, PGP groups public keys into bundles like this for convenience. The first signing key is the main identifier, but you can add and user other keys later, if you need.

The request to the key generator was for two keys pairs, one for DSA signing, another for ElGamal encryption. The "pub" line is for the DSA key, and the "sub" line is the identifying information for the public part of ElGamal key. The key has 2048 bits, and its short identifier is "530BAE58".

The "uid" applies to both keys, and it is simply a copy of what you entered during the key generation dialogue.

Let's return for a moment to the second line "public and secret key created and signed". What was signed and how? The public key "signed itself", and you can use this information to prove to people that you possess the private key. That is, the key really is part of a mathematically correct key pair.

PGP uses self-signed keys to bootstrap its trust model. People who see your self-signed PGP key can choose to trust it by using their own key to sign it. Similarly, you will need to sign the keys of your correspondents if you want to send encrypted email to them.

The PGP keys are part of a more complicated structure than this dialogue indicates. It is possible to look into the details using a command line request. Here we use the key identifier from the gen-key request:

```
gpg --edit-key B5565A34
Secret key is available.
pub  2048D/B5565A34   created: 2015-03-11   expires: 2017-03-10   usage: SC
                      trust: ultimate       validity: ultimate
sub  2048g/530BAE58   created: 2015-03-11   expires: 2017-03-10   usage: E
[ultimate] (1). Alice T. Smith <atsmith@example.com>

gpg> showpref
[ultimate] (1). Alice T. Smith <atsmith@example.com>
     Cipher: AES256, AES192, AES, CAST5, 3DES
     Digest: SHA256, SHA1, SHA384, SHA512, SHA224
     Compression: ZLIB, BZIP2, ZIP, Uncompressed
     Features: MDC, Keyserver no-modify
```

The second line shows that there is a secret key that can be used for signing. The third line shows that there is a 2048 DSA key, and it has the usage notation "SC" indicating that it is a signing key (S) and it can have more subkeys added to it (C). There is already a subkey of 2048 for ElGamal with usage "E" for encryption.

The "edit-key" option to gpg opens an interactive dialogue for managing key details. It should not be necessary to change anything, but it is interesting to look a the information saved with the key. The "showpref" subcommand reveals the auxiliary information that other people need to know when sending secure email to you. The "Cipher" section lists the symmetric ciphers that your PGP implementation supports; this is included because if a correspondent has software for additional ciphers, he needs to know that you cannot handle them. Similarly, the "Digest" list shows what hash functions you can use. The ciphers and hash functions are compatible with the security level of your public keys; correspondents should not try to communicate with inconsistent combinations. For example, you might be able to decrypt DES-encrypted messages, but the security level makes no sense when combined with your 2048 bit DSA and ElGamal.

If at some time in the future you learn that the security of 3DES is unreasonably low, you can edit your preferences for your keys and remove 3DES. Then you can export your key and send it to your correspondents. If they accept your new key, they will not use 3DES to encrypt messages to you.

Would you like some information about the private keys? You can issue the subcommand "toggle" and then see

```
ec  2048D/B5565A34   created: 2015-03-11   expires: 2017-03-10
ssb 2048g/530BAE58   created: 2015-03-11   expires: never
(1)  Alice T. Smith <atsmith@example.com>
```

That's not much information, but you can see that there is 2048 bit key for decryption ("D") and a 2048 bit key for verifying ("g"). Because verifying is the opposite of signing, you will not use your own verification key very often.

Somehow you will need to send your public keys to your correspondents. The "export" function packages your public key for sharing.

```
gpg -output aliceskey.gpg -export atsmith@example.com
or
gpg -output aliceskey.gpg -export B5565A34
```

The file "aliceskey.gpg" has the key and your identifying information and the cipher preferences—about 1600 byes of information, including the 256 byte (2048 bits) of the public key. You can send this as an attachment in an email message to your correspondents, or you can create something a little easier on the eyes by converting it to ascii characters in the style that PGP calls "ascii armor". The "-a" option on the export command creates the readable key block:

```
gpg -a --output aliceskey.asc --export B5565A34
```

Then you can view the aliceskey.asc file in a text editor and see something like:

```
-----BEGIN PGP PUBLIC KEY BLOCK-----
Version: GnuPG v1.4.11 (GNU/Linux)

mQMuBFUAzfwRCACutjD2SrHXiUtcvEpPujD8AZbfIidF5rx+40jjix+YpocZ/WZw
H5dGwDJXP8XtRNzzAuwmnS1Bis/A/carrqv/xDofvSLu2T+1jgMMrhu8p+HMJZ4H
0vzLnUx2aaLv806e139TlVhdjCGQ9kuSP0OT4X4cIDETISmVPUGDSyGfSNLmoTLp
mTn+dGZCQFiZf4ATMjrctHsXS7FwWvlf8L3eTGLT/j0ytPbE7Gdh00xQL76wcYIW
X9hYQT2UXsQRXCGiFdijeZXkDTnNUMiNdGoO8MsD7XolRbOh/DdXuscziRWqpvOR

...
=GoUk
-----END PGP PUBLIC KEY BLOCK-----
```

You can send this to anyone as an attachment or just ordinary text, and they should be able to "import" it into their key management system and use it to send email to you. When you correspond with someone new, it would be a good idea to sign the message with the signing key.

Suppose you want to use your PGP keys on a different computer. You might have generated your keys on your desktop machine, but you are going on a trip and you want to be able to read your encrypted email and send encrypted email to others when using your laptop machine or mobile device . This calls for exporting both your public and private key into a file. The following line causes the secret key for Alice to be written as an "ascii armored" file called "alicesecet.key".

```
gpg -a --output alicesecet.key --export-secret-keys B5565A34
```

The file looks like this:

```
-----BEGIN PGP PRIVATE KEY BLOCK-----
Version: GnuPG v1.4.11 (GNU/Linux)

lQN5BFUAzfwRCACutjD2SrHXiUtcvEpPujD8AZbfIidF5rx+40jjix+YpocZ/WZw
H5dGwDJXP8XtRNzzAuwmnS1Bis/A/carrqv/xDofvSLu2T+1jgMMrhu8p+HMJZ4H
0vzLnUx2aaLv806e139TlVhdjCGQ9kuSP0OT4X4cIDETISmVPUGDSyGfSNLmoTLp
mTn+dGZCQFiZf4ATMjrctHsXS7FwWvlf8L3eTGLT/j0ytPbE7Gdh00xQL76wcYIW

...
=pGMP
-----END PGP PRIVATE KEY BLOCK-----
```

This may seem insecure because it looks as though your secret key is unprotected. However, it is encrypted, and the decryption key is derived from the same passphrase that you used to create the keys when you ran the "gen-key" command above. You can safely move the private key file to other devices. You can import that file on other machines and then read encrypted email that was protected with the original key. What about your public keys? Those are also included in the private key block, and you do not need a separate command to bundle them up.

If your email client supports PGP keys, you should be able to use this key immediately to send signed and/or encrypted email to other PGP users. You may need to stop and restart your email client (such as Evolution or Thunderbird). You might also have to start and restart any key management application that handles PGP keys, particularly "GPG Key Access" on Mac OS and "Seahorse" or similar managers on Linux.

When Should You Get a New Key?

Whether you are using PGP or S/MIME, there two cogent reasons for getting a new key: no key should be used forever, and a new key can have attributes that are more secure than older keys. A key that has been in use for a number of years becomes suspect for the usual, mundane reasons that plague any form of information privacy on computers. Due to a defect or malware, the operating system might have disclosed the passphrase that unlocks the private key, or the private key might have been seen by malware examining the computer memory. Another problem might be that the passphrase was secure enough for several years, but modern search methods might have found it and used it to reveal the private key. The problems make it advisable to get a new key from time to time. A new key should supersede the older key, and therefore the older key should be revoked, if not immediately, at least after a short time of a month or two.

Even if the key has not reached its lifetime limit, the time might be ripe to get a key that is more secure. The key length might be increased if, for example, the current key is only 1024 bits for RSA. That may have been a reasonable choice when the computation time for using the key was a significant burden on a cell-phone, but a 2048 bit would be a good upgrade choice.

Even better than a longer RSA key, an elliptic curve key for DSA signing and ElGamal encryption might be in order. The elliptic curve algorithms are supported more and more widely, and your corrrespondents may be ready to switch to elliptic curve algorithms for their own use, too. For compatibility, you should not give up your RSA keys just yet, but forward looking users will be using elliptic curves.

Where Are the Certificates Kept?

On Linux and Unix systems, keys are kept in special subdirectories under the user's home directory. OpenSSL uses ".certs" for certificate storage, and GPG uses ". gnupg". If you have exported an S/MIME key file and want to install it on your local computer, you should create the .certs directory and put the key file there. Then you can import it with your email client.

The operating system keeps a list of trusted CA's for all users, and that can be changed by editing the system configuration files or through a key manager. It requires the "root" administrator permissions.

Chapter 5
Living with Encrypted Email

Managing email is definitely more complicated when it is encrypted. The price of privacy is eternal decryption! Users of encrypted email have to keep their private key handy. Keeping it available when traveling requires keeping that key secure, and that means protecting it with a passphrase. So, in addition to maintaining a password for the device itself, users need to keep track of another passphrase for the private key.

Almost any security expert will tell you that you need to keep your private data encrypted, even if it is on your own computer or mobile device. Almost anyone who is an expert in digital forensics will tell you that almost all passwords can be found somewhere on your computer or mobile device. Your encrypted email should remain encrypted when you aren't reading it, and your private key should be password protected when you aren't using it.

It is not possible to read encrypted email from a borrowed computer or a kiosk computer because the private key does not (and should not) exist there. This is a good thing altogether, but it means that even in an emergency you cannot read your encrypted email from someone else's computer. On the other hand, if you are reading your encrypted email over a public wifi connection, you don't have to worry about an electronic eavesdropper looking at your data connection.

Sometimes, though, you will want to save your email in its unencrypted form. Most email systems only decrypt the messages when you are reading them. After you move on to another message, the plaintext disappears. Some systems might have the option of keeping a decrypted copy, but that is not the normal case. If you need to search over all your old email for keywords in the message body, you won't find it in the encrypted messages unless the keyword is in the normal email headers: date, sender, subject.

It is possible to write software that will decrypt messages during the search process, and there might someday be practical systems that can perform searches without decrypting the email (that may sound impossible, but homomorphic encryption has this capability, its only drawback being that it is very, very slow). For the present time, though, most people will have to either explicitly save their decrypted messages or endure reduced search capability.

One very strange aspect of encryption is that you cannot read messages in the "Sent" folder. Those messages are encrypted in the key of the person receiving the

© The Author(s) 2015
H. Orman, *Encrypted Email*,
SpringerBriefs in Computer Science,
DOI 10.1007/978-3-319-21344-6_5

message, not the person sending the message. The sender can get around this problem by putting his own address in the "cc" line. When the sender receives a copy of his own message, it will be encrypted in his own key, and then he can read it. This is a nuisance, but it does put an extra level of protection on sensitive email—even the sender cannot read it without his private key.

This brings up the issue of sending an encrypted message to more than one person. Secure email systems handle this by including an encrypted copy of the symmetric cipher key for each recipient. The encrypted message body does not change, but the public key encryption of the symmetric cipher key is done once for each recipient's public key.

There are three problems with the multiple-recipients/multiple-keyblocks method. The first is that it introduces a few hundred bytes of data for each recipient, and this greatly increases the message size if there are many recipients.

When sending to a mailing list, the sender probably does not know all the recipients' email addresses, let alone their public keys. If the mailing list system has been designed for security, then all the public keys might be stored on the list server, and the server could handle the problem of adding a key block for each mailing list member. Therefore, the message must be encrypted using the public key of the secure mailing list server. The server can then extract the symmetric cipher key and add the public-key encrypted version for each user. That is when the third problem would probably arise: not all the recipients will support the same cipher algorithms. It might be necessary to encrypt the message in two or more different ciphers. Of course, if the email is an S/MIME message and you want the server to forward it to PGP users, the message has to be completely reprocessed.

More ideas on how to handle multiple destination messages in the IETF's definition of the message syntax for using multiple message keys in [31].

The best advice about forwarding encrypted email is to test before sending anything important. It is not easy to forward an encrypted message because the symmetric key is protected with the recipient's public key. In principle, forwarding could be done by simply extracting the symmetric key and re-encrypting it in the public key of a new recipient. The new recipient might not support the symmetric cipher of the original message, though, and the message would have to be re-encrypted. Even beyond this problem, though, there is a lurking chasm—different email system do different things, some useful, some not useful, and some dangerous.

On the other hand, forwarding signed email and preserving the signature is much less of a problem. If the signature is encoded with the message (i.e., not "detached"), then the message part can be attached to any other message without modification. All the information needed to verify it is contained in the S/MIME encoded part. PGP is similar in that all the necessary cryptographic information is contained in the PGP message "packets".

Should an encrypted message be automatically encrypted when forwarded? This decision usually has to be made by the user on a case-by-case basis, depending on the email client. The safest policy is to always preserve the privacy of a message, but this is easier with some clients than others.

The least useful thing that can happen with forwarded, encrypted email is to forward the encrypted part without modification. The recipient will not be able to decrypt the symmetric cipher key and will not be able to read the message. This is the most likely behavior from an ordinary email system. The encrypted message is a MIME or S/MIME part, and they are handled like any ordinary attachments—they are forwarded without modification.

Some systems will decrypt the message and re-encrypt it for the new recipient. For the reasons mentioned above, the encryption and key probably will be entirely new. This is the most useful thing that can happen.

Users who expect that encrypted email will remain encrypted when forwarded should run a few tests with their email client to make sure it behaves as they would expect. It is possible that the default action is to forward the message without encryption. Even if encryption is the default action, users should make sure that the software behaves properly when the new recipient's key is unknown. At least one system, in the past, would silently forward the unencrypted message in that case. The proper behavior is to alert the sender and offer the option to abort the send operation.

Among the other problems that encryption users will find is the problem of managing their private keys across multiple devices. The keys have to be moved securely, so they must be "exported" and protected with a passphrase. A good passphrase is essential to the longtime security of the email, and users should choose passphrases with at least 12 characters with uppercase and lowercase letters and numbers. Although it is tempting to choose something easy to remember, like "12 Characters", that is not a good idea. Pick something that is barely memorable. For an excellent set of principles to help with memorization of difficult sequences, see [12].

After exporting the keys into a file (which will have the filename extension "p12" for S/MIME or "asc" for PGP), the user can send the file to himself as an attachment. This email does not need encryption. Then, he can read the email on a new device and import the file, usually by clicking on it and entering the pass-phrase. The same thing can be achieved by saving the attachment as a local file and importing it using a key manager.

The MIME and S/MIME headers are general enough to describe complex messages with multiple parts, each protected with different methods and different keys. For example, a message might have one attachment signed with your own key, another part that you received from someone else, signed with their key, a part encrypted with PGP, another encrypted with S/MIME methods, and a part with an X.509 certificate for someone else, and a part with a PGP key that you signed. However, you will not find an email client that can construct such messages. Most email clients can deal with messages that are slightly more complicated that what they can generate, but none are capable of handling the full spectrum of what S/MIME and MIME can describe.

Although you will not find a fully automatic process for building complex messages, they can still be put together through command line construction of the parts. Each part can be protected with security enhancements and then added to the outgoing message as an attachment. The recipient will have to undo the operations on each part using command line operations. It is probably easier to send separate messages than to construct an omnibus message!

There is one kind of complex message that is explicitly supported by S/MIME. A message can have nested headers, for example, signed and then encrypted, which is supported by all email clients. What is not commonly known is that the nesting can continue to arbitrary depth. The "triple wrapped" message is particularly useful. The data is first signed, then encrypted, and then signed. More accurately, it is signed, encrypted, prepended with additional header information or attribute information, and then signed. The second signature does not have to use the same key as the first (innermost) part. The result is a message that has some cleartext, authenticated data. This allows a gateway mail handler to be entrusted with a signing key for the outermost layer, but it does not have to be trusted with the potentially more sensitive encryption and inner signing keys. Moreover, the receiving mail handler can use the cleartext information as part of delivery. After the message is routed, for example, over a secure network, the final recipient can use his own key to read the protected content, and he can determine the authenticity of the content as signed by his direct correspondent.

Outlook supports triple-wrapping. Other clients may be able to read triple-wrapped messages but are unable to create them.

RFC 2634, Enhanced Security Services for S/MIME, explains the multiple layering and three other interesting services that can be encoded in S/MIME. These are not widely supported, but most users will at one time or another think two of them could be of use. Secure delivery receipts, for example, partially solve the problem of wondering if the mail got lost. If it was received by the proper end user system, the receipt will attest to that fact. Sending secure email to a mailing list is another useful service, and the RFC describes some of the gory details of how to avoid several pitfalls (such as delivery loops) while still allowing encryption for each recipient. The fourth service, security labels, is very important to military organizations, but it has limited appeal generally.

Chapter 6
Conclusion

The need for secure communication remains the same since ancient times. The military, businesses, and individuals need privacy in order to function effectively. There can be no "checks and balances" if communication cannot be kept private. Most human institutions are built on the assumption that some things can remain guarded, at least for a limited period of time. In today's era of pervasive and immediate communication, privacy remains as important as ever.

The evolution of encrypted email on the Internet has been slow, perhaps slower than any other communication protocol. Today, there are two protocol suites to choose from, PGP and S/MIME, and both are generally supported on all common computing platforms. Nonetheless, there are impediments to using encryption that have not yet been addressed by open source developers.

The bifurcation between S/MIME and PGP, between X.509 certificates and a web of signed keys, is a problem that interferes with any attempts to have secure email "go viral". Keys have to be exchanged, and users will need two keys, at least, to participate with the full spectrum of email systems. The keys must be moved to new devices. The multiplicative factor of these small tasks builds up, keeping secure email users in small disconnected islands rather than deeply connected. Today's Internet is all about connections, as the rampant success of social media has shown. We need to have security that is a constant companion to our social connections.

Secure email technology will be inaccessible to the average user until the rough edges come off. That will only happen when enough people use it to cause a spate of tool building and dedicated attention to interoperability. The long, drawn out standardization process that contributed to the slow uptake on S/MIME did, ultimately, result in a comprehensive definition of how to implement and use secure email. The problems today seem to be centered on key access and the surrounding management issues. We all need key management for our Internet-based activities, and there should be a market for secure and easy key management.

Users who turn to the "advanced" tab and enable email security are taking the first small step on a long journey, but the footprints that hit this particular trail may well shorten the path for those who follow.

© The Author(s) 2015
H. Orman, *Encrypted Email*,
SpringerBriefs in Computer Science,
DOI 10.1007/978-3-319-21344-6_6

Appendix 1
Supported Algorithms for PGP and OpenSSL

GPG Version 1.6 supported algorithms:

Public key	RSA, RSA-E, RSA-S, ELG-E, DSA
Symmetric ciphers	3DES, CAST5, BLOWFISH, AES, AES192, AES256, TWOFISH, CAMELLIA128, CAMELLIA192, CAMELLIA256
Hash function (MDC)	MD5, SHA1, RIPEMD160, SHA256, SHA384, SHA512, SHA224

There are OpenPGP extensions for elliptic curve methods that offer much faster public key methods while retaining excellent security. The acceptance of elliptic curves has been moving very slowly, but GPG version 2 now supports them.

GPG Version 2.1.2 supported algorithms

Public key	RSA, ELG, DSA, ECDH, ECDSA, EdDSA
Symmetric ciphers	IDEA, 3DES, CAST5, BLOWFISH, AES, AES192, AES256, TWOFISH, CAMELLIA128, CAMELLIA192, CAMELLIA256
Hash function (MDC)	SHA1, RIPEMD160, SHA256, SHA384, SHA512, SHA224

OpenSSL also has a wide range of ciphers. These are arranged into "cipher suites" in which the three essential algorithms, public key, symmetric cipher, and hash function, are specified as a group.

OpenSSL 0.9.8o 01 Jun 2010

Suite name	vr	Key exchange	Authentication, encryption, hash	Export?
DHE-RSA-AES256-SHA	3	DH	Au=RSA Enc=AES(256) Mac=SHA1	
DHE-DSS-AES256-SHA	3	DH	Au=DSS Enc=AES(256) Mac=SHA1	

(continued)

© The Author(s) 2015
H. Orman, *Encrypted Email*,
SpringerBriefs in Computer Science,
DOI 10.1007/978-3-319-21344-6

Suite name	vr	Key exchange	Authentication, encryption, hash	Export?
AES256-SHA	3	RSA	Au=RSA Enc=AES(256) Mac=SHA1	
EDH-RSA-DES-CBC3-SHA	3	DH	Au=RSA Enc=3DES (168) Mac=SHA1	
EDH-DSS-DES-CBC3-SHA	3	DH	Au=DSS Enc=3DES (168) Mac=SHA1	
DES-CBC3-SHA	3	RSA	Au=RSA Enc=3DES (168) Mac=SHA1	
DES-CBC3-MD5	2	RSA	Au=RSA Enc=3DES (168) Mac=MD5	
DHE-RSA-AES128-SHA	3	DH	Au=RSA Enc=AES(128) Mac=SHA1	
DHE-DSS-AES128-SHA	3	DH	Au=DSS Enc=AES(128) Mac=SHA1	
AES128-SHA	3	RSA	Au=RSA Enc=AES(128) Mac=SHA1	
RC2-CBC-MD5	2	RSA	Au=RSA Enc=RC2(128) Mac=MD5	
RC4-SHA	3	RSA	Au=RSA Enc=RC4(128) Mac=SHA1	
RC4-MD5	3	RSA	Au=RSA Enc=RC4(128) Mac=MD5	
RC4-MD5	2	RSA	Au=RSA Enc=RC4(128) Mac=MD5	
EDH-RSA-DES-CBC-SHA	3	DH	Au=RSA Enc=DES(56) Mac=SHA1	
EDH-DSS-DES-CBC-SHA	3	DH	Au=DSS Enc=DES(56) Mac=SHA1	
DES-CBC-SHA	3	RSA	Au=RSA Enc=DES(56) Mac=SHA1	
DES-CBC-MD5	2	RSA	Au=RSA Enc=DES(56) Mac=MD5	
EXP-EDH-RSA-DES-CBC-SHA	3	DH(512)	Au=RSA Enc=DES(40) Mac=SHA1	Yes
EXP-EDH-DSS-DES-CBC-SHA	3	DH(512)	Au=DSS Enc=DES(40) Mac=SHA1	Yes
EXP-DES-CBC-SHA	3	RSA (512)	Au=RSA Enc=DES(40) Mac=SHA1	Yes
EXP-RC2-CBC-MD5	3	RSA (512)	Au=RSA Enc=RC2(40) Mac=MD5	Yes
EXP-RC2-CBC-MD5	2	RSA (512)	Au=RSA Enc=RC2(40) Mac=MD5	Yes
EXP-RC4-MD5	3	RSA (512)	Au=RSA Enc=RC4(40) Mac=MD5	Yes
EXP-RC4-MD5	2	RSA (512)	Au=RSA Enc=RC4(40) Mac=MD5	Yes

OpenSSL v3 1.0.1f 6 Jan 2014

Suite name	Key exchange	Authentication, encryption, hash
ECDHE-RSA-AES256-SHA	ECDH	Au=RSA Enc=AES(256) Mac=SHA1
ECDHE-ECDSA-AES256-SHA	ECDH	Au=ECDSA Enc=AES(256) Mac=SHA1
SRP-DSS-AES-256-CBC-SHA	SRP	Au=DSS Enc=AES(256) Mac=SHA1
SRP-RSA-AES-256-CBC-SHA	SRP	Au=RSA Enc=AES(256) Mac=SHA1
SRP-AES-256-CBC-SHA	SRP	Au=SRP Enc=AES(256) Mac=SHA1
DHE-RSA-AES256-SHA	DH	RSA Enc=AES(256) Mac=SHA1
DHE-DSS-AES256-SHA	DH	DSS Enc=AES(256) Mac=SHA1
DHE-RSA-CAMELLIA256-SHA	DH	RSA Enc=Camellia(256) Mac=SHA1
DHE-DSS-CAMELLIA256-SHA	DH	DSS Enc=Camellia(256) Mac=SHA1
ECDH-RSA-AES256-SHA	ECDH/RSA	Au=ECDH Enc=AES(256) Mac=SHA1
ECDH-ECDSA-AES256-SHA	ECDH/ECDSA	Au=ECDH Enc=AES(256) Mac=SHA1
AES256-SHA	RSA	RSA Enc=AES(256) Mac=SHA1
CAMELLIA256-SHA	RSA	RSA Enc=Camellia(256) Mac=SHA1
PSK-AES256-CBC-SHA	PSK	Au=PSK Enc=AES(256) Mac=SHA1
ECDHE-RSA-DES-CBC3-SHA	ECDH	Au=RSA Enc=3DES(168) Mac=SHA1
ECDHE-ECDSA-DES-CBC3-SHA	ECDH	Au=ECDSA Enc=3DES(168) Mac=SHA1
SRP-DSS-3DES-EDE-CBC-SHA	SRP	Au=DSS Enc=3DES(168) Mac=SHA1
SRP-RSA-3DES-EDE-CBC-SHA	SRP	Au=RSA Enc=3DES(168) Mac=SHA1
SRP-3DES-EDE-CBC-SHA	SRP	Au=SRP Enc=3DES(168) Mac=SHA1
EDH-RSA-DES-CBC3-SHA	DH	Au=RSA Enc=3DES(168) Mac=SHA1
EDH-DSS-DES-CBC3-SHA	DH	Au=DSS Enc=3DES(168) Mac=SHA1
ECDH-RSA-DES-CBC3-SHA	ECDH/RSA	Au=ECDH Enc=3DES(168) Mac=SHA1
ECDH-ECDSA-DES-CBC3-SHA	ECDH/ECDSA	Au=ECDH Enc=3DES(168) Mac=SHA1

(continued)

Suite name	Key exchange	Authentication, encryption, hash
DES-CBC3-SHA	RSA	Au=RSA Enc=3DES(168) Mac=SHA1
PSK-3DES-EDE-CBC-SHA	PSK	PSK Enc=3DES(168) Mac=SHA1
ECDHE-RSA-AES128-SHA	ECDH	Au=RSA Enc=AES(128) Mac=SHA1
ECDHE-ECDSA-AES128-SHA	ECDH	Au=ECDSA Enc=AES(128) Mac=SHA1
SRP-DSS-AES-128-CBC-SHA	SRP	DSS Enc=AES(128) Mac=SHA1
SRP-RSA-AES-128-CBC-SHA	SRP	RSA Enc=AES(128) Mac=SHA1
SRP-AES-128-CBC-SHA	SRP	SRP Enc=AES(128) Mac=SHA1
DHE-RSA-AES128-SHA	DH	RSA Enc=AES(128) Mac=SHA1
DHE-DSS-AES128-SHA	DH	DSS Enc=AES(128) Mac=SHA1
DHE-RSA-SEED-SHA	DH	RSA Enc=SEED(128) Mac=SHA1
DHE-DSS-SEED-SHA	DH	DSS Enc=SEED(128) Mac=SHA1
DHE-RSA-CAMELLIA128-SHA	DH	RSA Enc=Camellia(128) Mac=SHA1
DHE-DSS-CAMELLIA128-SHA	DH	DSS Enc=Camellia(128) Mac=SHA1
ECDH-RSA-AES128-SHA	ECDH/RSA	Au=ECDH Enc=AES(128) Mac=SHA1
ECDH-ECDSA-AES128-SHA	ECDH/ECDSA	Au=ECDH Enc=AES(128) Mac=SHA1
AES128-SHA	RSA	RSA Enc=AES(128) Mac=SHA1
SEED-SHA	RSA	RSA Enc=SEED(128) Mac=SHA1
CAMELLIA128-SHA	RSA	RSA Enc=Camellia(128) Mac=SHA1
PSK-AES128-CBC-SHA	PSK	PSK Enc=AES(128) Mac=SHA1
ECDHE-RSA-RC4-SHA	ECDH	Au=RSA Enc=RC4(128) Mac=SHA1
ECDHE-ECDSA-RC4-SHA	ECDH	Au=ECDSA Enc=RC4(128) Mac=SHA1
ECDH-RSA-RC4-SHA	ECDH/RSA	Au=ECDH Enc=RC4(128) Mac=SHA1
ECDH-ECDSA-RC4-SHA	ECDH/ECDSA	Au=ECDH Enc=RC4(128) Mac=SHA1
RC4-SHA	RSA	RSA Enc=RC4(128) Mac=SHA1
RC4-MD5	RSA	RSA Enc=RC4(128) Mac=MD5
PSK-RC4-SHA	PSK	PSK Enc=RC4(128) Mac=SHA1
EDH-RSA-DES-CBC-SHA	DH	RSA Enc=DES(56) Mac=SHA1
EDH-DSS-DES-CBC-SHA	DH	DSS Enc=DES(56) Mac=SHA1
DES-CBC-SHA	RSA	RSA Enc=DES(56) Mac=SHA1
EXP-EDH-RSA-DES-CBC-SHA[a]	DH(512)	Au=RSA Enc=DES(40) Mac=SHA1

(continued)

Suite name	Key exchange	Authentication, encryption, hash
EXP-EDH-DSS-DES-CBC-SHA[a]	DH(512)	Au=DSS Enc=DES(40) Mac=SHA1
EXP-DES-CBC-SHA[a]	RSA(512)	Au=RSA Enc=DES(40) Mac=SHA1
EXP-RC2-CBC-MD5[a]	RSA(512)	RSA Enc=RC2(40) Mac=MD5
EXP-RC4-MD5[a]	RSA(512)	RSA Enc=RC4(40) Mac=MD5

[a]Exportable

Appendix 2
ASN.1 Definition of an S/MIME Message Part

This gives some idea of how the Cryptographic Message Syntax is embodied in S/MIME messages. The first line shows the sequence of values that indicate that what follows is encoded for S/MIME version 3.1. From IETF RFC5911, "New ASN.1 Modules for Cryptographic Message Syntax (CMS) and S/MIME", by P. Hoffman and J. Schaad, June 2010.

```
SecureMimeMessageV3dot1
  { iso(1) member-body(2) us(840) rsadsi(113549)
      pkcs(1) pkcs-9(9) smime(16) modules(0) msg-v3dot1(21) }

DEFINITIONS IMPLICIT TAGS ::=
BEGIN

IMPORTS
-- Cryptographic Message Syntax
    SubjectKeyIdentifier, IssuerAndSerialNumber,
    RecipientKeyIdentifier
        FROM    CryptographicMessageSyntax
                { iso(1) member-body(2) us(840) rsadsi(113549)
                  pkcs(1) pkcs-9(9) smime(16) modules(0) cms-2001(14) };


-- id-aa is the arc with all new authenticated and unauthenticated
-- attributes produced the by S/MIME Working Group

id-aa OBJECT IDENTIFIER ::= {iso(1) member-body(2) usa(840)
        rsadsi(113549) pkcs(1) pkcs-9(9) smime(16) attributes(2)}

-- S/MIME Capabilities provides a method of broadcasting the symmetric
-- capabilities understood.  Algorithms SHOULD be ordered by
-- preference and grouped by type

smimeCapabilities OBJECT IDENTIFIER ::=
    {iso(1) member-body(2) us(840) rsadsi(113549) pkcs(1) pkcs-9(9) 15}
```

© The Author(s) 2015
H. Orman, *Encrypted Email*,
SpringerBriefs in Computer Science,
DOI 10.1007/978-3-319-21344-6

```
SMIMECapability ::= SEQUENCE {
   capabilityID OBJECT IDENTIFIER,
   parameters ANY DEFINED BY capabilityID OPTIONAL }

SMIMECapabilities ::= SEQUENCE OF SMIMECapability

-- Encryption Key Preference provides a method of broadcasting the
-- preferred encryption certificate.

id-aa-encrypKeyPref OBJECT IDENTIFIER ::= {id-aa 11}

SMIMEEncryptionKeyPreference ::= CHOICE {
   issuerAndSerialNumber    [0] IssuerAndSerialNumber,
   receipentKeyId           [1] RecipientKeyIdentifier,
   subjectAltKeyIdentifier  [2] SubjectKeyIdentifier
}
```

Appendix 3
IETF Documents for S/MIME Mail Security

This information is from the IETF website in the section for the smime working group. It shows the complete history of documents produced by the group. Note that some documents have several versions, and some have been rendered obsolete.

Document	Date	Status
RFC 2630 Cryptographic Message Syntax	1999-06 60 pages	Proposed Standard RFC Obsoleted by RFC3369, RFC3370 IETF RFC stream
RFC 2631 Diffie-Hellman Key Agreement Method	1999-06 13 pages	Proposed Standard RFC IETF RFC stream
RFC 2632 S/MIME Version 3 Certificate Handling	1999-06 13 pages	Proposed Standard RFC Obsoleted by RFC3850 IETF RFC stream
RFC 2633 S/MIME Version 3 Message Specification	1999-06 32 pages	Proposed Standard RFC Obsoleted by RFC3851 IETF RFC stream
RFC 2634 Enhanced Security Services for S/MIME	1999-06 58 pages	Proposed Standard RFC Updated by RFC5035 IETF RFC stream
RFC 2785 Methods for Avoiding the "Small-Subgroup" Attacks on the Diffie-Hellman Key Agreement Method for S/MIME	2000-03 11 pages	Informational RFC IETF RFC stream
RFC 2876 Use of the KEA and SKIPJACK Algorithms in CMS	2000-07 13 pages	Informational RFC IETF RFC stream

(continued)

© The Author(s) 2015
H. Orman, *Encrypted Email*,
SpringerBriefs in Computer Science,
DOI 10.1007/978-3-319-21344-6

Document	Date	Status
RFC 2984 Use of the CAST-128 Encryption Algorithm in CMS	2000-10 6 pages	Proposed Standard RFC IETF RFC stream
RFC 3058 Use of the IDEA Encryption Algorithm in CMS	2001-02 8 pages	Informational RFC IETF RFC stream
RFC 3114 Implementing Company Classification Policy with the S/MIME Security Label	2002-05 14 pages	Informational RFC IETF RFC stream
RFC 3125 Electronic Signature Policies	2001-09 44 pages	Experimental RFC WG Document
RFC 3126 Electronic Signature Formats for long term electronic signatures	2001-09 84 pages	Informational RFC Obsoleted by RFC5126 WG Document
RFC 3183 Domain Security Services using S/MIME	2001-10 24 pages	Experimental RFC IETF RFC stream
RFC 3185 Reuse of CMS Content Encryption Keys	2001-10 10 pages	Proposed Standard RFC IETF RFC stream
RFC 3211 Password-based Encryption for CMS	2001-12 17 pages	Proposed Standard RFC Obsoleted by RFC3369, RFC3370 IETF RFC stream
RFC 3217 Triple-DES and RC2 Key Wrapping	2001-12 9 pages	Informational RFC IETF RFC stream
RFC 3218 Preventing the Million Message Attack on Cryptographic Message Syntax	2002-01 7 pages	Informational RFC IETF RFC stream
RFC 3274 Compressed Data Content Type for Cryptographic Message Syntax (CMS)	2002-06 6 pages	Proposed Standard RFC IETF RFC stream
RFC 3278 Use of Elliptic Curve Cryptography (ECC) Algorithms in Cryptographic Message Syntax (CMS)	2002-05 16 pages	Informational RFC Obsoleted by RFC5753 IETF RFC stream
RFC 3369 Cryptographic Message Syntax (CMS)	2002-09 52 pages	Proposed Standard RFC Obsoleted by RFC3852 IETF RFC stream
RFC 3370 Cryptographic Message Syntax (CMS) Algorithms Errata	2002-09 24 pages	Proposed Standard RFC Updated by RFC5754 IETF RFC stream

(continued)

Document	Date	Status
RFC 3394 Advanced Encryption Standard (AES) [2] Key Wrap Algorithm Errata	2002-10 41 pages	Informational RFC IETF RFC stream
RFC 3537 Wrapping a Hashed Message Authentication Code (HMAC) key with a Triple-Data Encryption Standard (DES) [5] Key or an Advanced Encryption Standard (AES) Key	2003-05 9 pages	Proposed Standard RFC IETF RFC stream
RFC 3560 Use of the RSAES-OAEP Key Transport Algorithm in Cryptographic Message Syntax (CMS)	2003-07 18 pages	Proposed Standard RFC IETF RFC stream
RFC 3565 Use of the Advanced Encryption Standard (AES) Encryption Algorithm in Cryptographic Message Syntax (CMS)	2003-07 14 pages	Proposed Standard RFC IETF RFC stream
RFC 3657 Use of the Camellia Encryption Algorithm in Cryptographic Message Syntax (CMS)	2004-01 14 pages	Proposed Standard RFC IETF RFC stream
RFC 3850 (was draft-ietf-smime-rfc2632bis) Secure/Multipurpose Internet Mail Extensions (S/MIME) Version 3.1 Certificate Handling	2004-07 16 pages	Proposed Standard RFC Obsoleted by RFC5750 IETF RFC stream
RFC 3851 Secure/Multipurpose Internet Mail Extensions (S/MIME) Version 3.1 Message Specification	2004-07 36 pages	Proposed Standard RFC Obsoleted by RFC5751 IETF RFC stream
RFC 3852 Cryptographic Message Syntax (CMS)	2004-07 56 pages	Proposed Standard RFC Obsoleted by RFC5652 Updated by RFC4853, RFC5083 IETF RFC stream
RFC 3854 Securing X.400 Content with Secure/Multipurpose Internet Mail Extensions (S/MIME)	2004-07 15 pages	Proposed Standard RFC IETF RFC stream
RFC 3855 Transporting Secure/Multipurpose Internet Mail Extensions (S/MIME) Objects in X.400	2004-07 12 pages	Proposed Standard RFC IETF RFC stream
RFC 4010 Use of the SEED Encryption Algorithm in Cryptographic Message Syntax (CMS)	2005-02 13 pages	Proposed Standard RFC IETF RFC stream
RFC 4056 Use of the RSASSA-PSS Signature Algorithm in Cryptographic Message Syntax (CMS)	2005-06 6 pages	Proposed Standard RFC WG Document

(continued)

Document	Date	Status
RFC 4134 Examples of S/MIME Messages	2005-07 136 pages	Informational RFC IETF RFC stream
RFC 4262 X.509 Certificate Extension for Secure/Multipurpose Internet Mail Extensions (S/MIME) Capabilities	2005-12 5 pages	Proposed Standard RFC IETF RFC stream
RFC 4490 Using the GOST 28147-89, GOST R 34.11-94, GOST R 34.10-94, and GOST R 34.10-2001 Algorithms with Cryptographic Message Syntax (CMS)	2006-05 29 pages	Proposed Standard RFC IETF RFC stream
RFC 4853 Cryptographic Message Syntax (CMS) Multiple Signer Clarification	2007-04 5 pages	Proposed Standard RFC IETF RFC stream
RFC 5035 Enhanced Security Services (ESS) Update: Adding CertID Algorithm Agility	2007-08 17 pages	Proposed Standard RFC IETF RFC stream
RFC 5083 Cryptographic Message Syntax (CMS) Authenticated-Enveloped-Data Content Type	2007-11 10 pages	Proposed Standard RFC IETF RFC stream
RFC 5084 Using AES-CCM and AES-GCM Authenticated Encryption in the Cryptographic Message Syntax (CMS)	2007-11 11 pages	Proposed Standard RFC IETF RFC stream
RFC 5126 CMS Advanced Electronic Signatures (CAdES)	2008-03 141 pages	Informational RFC WG Document
RFC 5275 CMS Symmetric Key Management and Distribution	2008-06 89 pages	Proposed Standard RFC IETF RFC stream
RFC 5408 Identity-Based Encryption Architecture and Supporting Data Structures	2009-01 30 pages	Informational RFC IETF RFC stream
RFC 5409 Using the Boneh-Franklin and Boneh-Boyen Identity-Based Encryption Algorithms with the Cryptographic Message Syntax (CMS)	2009-01 13 pages	Informational RFC IETF RFC stream
RFC 562 Cryptographic Message Syntax (CMS)	2009-09 56 pages	Internet Standard RFC IETF RFC stream
RFC 5750 Secure/Multipurpose Internet Mail Extensions (S/MIME) Version 3.2 Certificate Handling	2010-01 21 pages	Proposed Standard RFC IETF RFC stream
RFC 5751 Secure/Multipurpose Internet Mail Extensions (S/MIME) Version 3.2 Message Specification	2010-01 45 pages	Proposed Standard RFC IETF RFC stream
RFC 5752 Multiple Signatures in Cryptographic Message Syntax (CMS) Errata	2010-01 17 pages	Proposed Standard RFC WG Document

(continued)

Document	Date	Status
RFC 5753 Use of Elliptic Curve Cryptography (ECC) Algorithms in Cryptographic Message Syntax (CMS)	2010-01 61 pages	Informational RFC IETF RFC stream
RFC 5754 Using SHA2 Algorithms with Cryptographic Message Syntax Errata	2010-01 10 pages	Proposed Standard RFC IETF RFC stream
RFC 5911 New ASN.1 Modules for Cryptographic Message Syntax (CMS) and S/MIME Errata	2010-06 59 pages	Informational RFC Updated by RFC6268 IETF RFC stream
RFC 5990 Use of the RSA-KEM Key Transport Algorithm in the Cryptographic Message Syntax (CMS)	2010-09 27 pages	Proposed Standard RFC IETF RFC stream
Related documents		
draft-melnikov-smime-header-signing-02 Considerations for protecting Email header with S/MIME	2015-04-03 6 pages	I-D Exists
draft-melnikov-smime-msa-to-mda-04 Domain-based signing and encryption using S/MIME	2014-03-05 26 pages	Waiting for Writeup for 414 days Proposed Standard Submitted to IESG for Publication

Appendix: OpenPGP, Internet RFCs

Document	Date	Status
RFC 2440 OpenPGP Message Format	1998-11 65 pages	Proposed Standard RFC Obsoleted by RFC4880 IETF RFC stream
RFC 3156 MIME Security with OpenPGP	2001-08 15 pages	Proposed Standard RFC IETF RFC stream
RFC 4880 OpenPGP Message Format	2007-11 90 pages	Proposed Standard RFC Updated by RFC5581 IETF RFC stream
Related documents		
draft-atkins-openpgp-algebraic-eraser-04 Using Algebraic Eraser (AEDH) in OpenPGP	2015-01-14 12 pages	
draft-atkins-openpgp-device-certificates-02 OpenPGP Extensions for Device Certificates	2014-12-08 9 pages	
draft-vb-openpgp-linked-ids-00 Linked Identites for OpenPGP	2015-04-15 New 9 pages	
draft-vb-openpgp-uri-attribute-00 URI Attributes for OpenPGP	2015-04-11 New 4 pages	

Bibliography

1. Adams C, Lloyd S (1999) Understanding public-key infrastructure: concepts, standards, and deployment considerations. New Riders Publishing. ISBN 1-57870-166-x
2. Advanced Encryption Standard (2001) Federal information processing standards publication 197, November 26
3. Bell DE, LaPadula LJ (1974) Secure Computer Systems. Mathematical foundations and model M74–244, MITRE Corp., Bedford, Mass
4. Boneh D, Franklin M (2003) Identity based encryption from the Weil pairing. SIAM J Comput 32(3):586–615. Extended abstract in proc. of Crypto '2001, LNCS 2139:213–229. Springer-Verlag. 2001
5. Data Encryption Standard (1977) NIST, FIPS-46
6. Deutsch DP, Dodds DW (1979) Hermes system overview, BBN report No. 4115
7. Diffie W, Hellman ME (1977) Special feature exhaustive cryptanalysis of the NBS data encryption standard. Computer 10(6):74–84
8. Diffie W, Hellman ME (1976) New directions in cryptography. IEEE transactions on information theory, vol IT-22, No. 6
9. Dingledine R, Mathewson N, Syverson P (2004) Tor: the second-generation onion router. In: Proceedings of the 13th conference on USENIX security symposium, vol 13. USENIX Association, San Diego, CA, pp 21
10. FIPS (2009) Digital signature standard, NIST, FIPS publication 186–3. [This has been superseded by FIPS 186-4]
11. FIPS (2014) NIST, Draft FIPS 202, SHA-3 standard: permutation-based hash and extendable-output functions
12. Foer J (2012) Moonwalking with Einstein: the art and science of remembering everything. Penguin Books, Reprint edition, Paperback: 320 pages. ISBN-10: 9780143120537, ISBN-13: 978-0143120537, ASIN: 0143120530
13. Heninger N, Durumeric Z, Wustrow E, Halderman JA (2012) Mining your {p}s and {q}s: {d}etection of widespread weak keys in network devices. In: Proceedings of the 21st {USENIX} security symposium
14. Hoffman P (2002) IETF RFC 3207, SMTP service extension for secure SMTP over transport layer security
15. Housley R (2009) IETF RFC5652, cryptographic message syntax
16. Kahn D (1967) The code breakers. MacMillan Publishing Company. ISBN 0-020560460-0
17. Kallander JW, Goodwin NC, Hosmer S, Smith C, Fralick D (1979) Military message experiment, mid experiment report. Memorandum rept. Nov 78-Mar 79, DTIC (Defense Techical Information Center) Accession Number: ADA079889
18. Kent ST (1995) Internet Privacy Enhanced Mail. In: Marshall D, Abrams SJ, Podell HJ (eds) Information security: an integrated collection of essay's. IEEE Computer Society Press, Los Alamitos, California, USA. ISBN 0-8186-3662-9, LoC CIP: 94-20899, DDN: QA76.9. A25I5415

© The Author(s) 2015
H. Orman, *Encrypted Email*,
SpringerBriefs in Computer Science,
DOI 10.1007/978-3-319-21344-6

19. Kohnfelder L (1978) Towards a practical public key system, MIT. B.S. Thesis
20. Kurtz A. What apple missed to fix in iOS 7.1.1. http://www.andreas-kurtz.de/2014/04/what-apple-missed-to-fix-in-ios-711.html
21. Linde RL, Chaney PE (1966) Operational management of time-sharing systems in ACM '66: Proceedings of the 1966 21st National Conference, pp 149–159. ACM, New York, NY. doi:10.1145/800256. 810691
22. Linn J (1993) IETF RFC 1421, privacy enhancement for internet electronic mail: part i: message encryption and authentication procedures
23. Matsui M, Nakajima J, Moriai S (2004) IETF RFC 3713, a description of the Camellia Encryption Algorithm
24. Merkle R, Hellman M (1978) Hiding information and signatures in trapdoor knapsacks. Inf Theory, IEEE Trans 24(5):525–530
25. Nelson R, Heimann J (1990) Advances in cryptology—CRYPTO' 89 proceedings. In: Brassard G (eds) Lecture notes in computer science, SDNS architecture and end-to-end encryption, vol 435. Springer, New York, pp 356–366
26. Ramsdell B, Turner S (2010) IETF RFC 5751, secure/multipurpose internet mail extensions (S/MIME) version 3.2, message specification
27. Rivest RL, Shamir A, Adleman L (1978) A method for obtaining digital signatures and public-key cryptosystems. Commun ACM 21(2):120–126
28. Schneier B (1996) Applied cryptography, 2nd edn. John Wiley and Sons. ISBN 0-471-12845-7
29. Short history of study group 17 (2013) http://www.itu.int/en/ITU-T/studygroups/com17/Pages/history.aspx
30. Sibert WO, Baldwin RW (2007) The multics encipher_Algorithm. Cryptologia, Taylor and Francis Group, LLC 31(4):292–304. ISSN: 0161-1194; doi: 10.1080/01611190701506105
31. Turner S (2008) IETF RFC 5275, CMS symmetric key management and distribution
32. Whitten A, Tygar JD (1999) Why Johnny can't encrypt: a usability evaluation of PGP 5.0. In: Proceedings of the 8th conference on USENIX security symposium, vol 8. USENIX Association, Washington, DC, pp 14

Printed in the United States
By Bookmasters